SILENCE MEANS SECURITY
Secrets of a WWII Code-Breaking WAC

BARBARA NICODEMUS

Moonshine Cove Publishing, LLC
Abbeville, South Carolina U.S.A.

All rights reserved. No part of this book may be reproduced in whole or in part without written permission from the publisher except by reviewers who may quote brief excerpts in connection with a review in a newspaper, magazine or electronic publication; nor may any part of this book be reproduced, stored in a retrieval system or transmitted in any form or by any means electronic, mechanical, photocopying, recording or any other means, without written permission from the publisher.

This book shall not be lent, resold, hired out or otherwise circulated without the publisher's prior consent in any form of binding or cover other than that in which it is published. For information about permission to reproduce selections from this book, write to Moonshine Cove Publishing, 150 Willow Pt, Abbeville, SC 29620.

ISBN: 978-1-937327-76-7
Library of Congress Control Number: 2015951688
Copyright © 2015 by Barbara Nicodemus

Interior & cover design by Moonshine Cove staff; author photo by Barbara Pfaffe; cover photo WWII U.S. Army poster.

Dedication

To My Mom and the Women of the 5205th

A CODE-BREAKING WAC IN THE PACIFIC DURING WWII — DECIPHERING JAPANESE SECRETS WHILE COPING WITH A BITTERSWEET LOVE.

Nineteen-year-old Billie Jean had no idea when she walked into the Army Recruiting office in 1943 that in less than a year she would be breaking code in the Southwest Pacific. Her WWII military service in the Women's Army Corps would take her from her home in West Texas to assignments in Australia, New Guinea and the Philippines. While her wanderlust and volunteer spirit got her to the Pacific, her intelligence and attention to detail got her hand-picked for an all women select cryptologic field unit. Billie Jean struggles to decipher enemy secrets while confronting all the dangers of love and war.

The selfless service and contribution of U.S. women serving in the Signal Intelligence Service during the Second World War is relatively unknown. Cryptanalyst, Genevieve Grotjan Feinstein's discovery was the key to breaking the "Purple" Japanese Diplomatic code which was crucial in allowing the Allies to win the war in the Pacific. Much of the highly secretive work was done by women back home and in the field. Follow the untold story of WWII Signal Intelligence WACS serving in the Southwest Pacific through the eyes Billie Jean Nicodemus, one of their own.

"I was particularly impressed by how you captured both the intensity of war and your mother's drive to make a difference. I was also struck how your mom matured over her experiences. She was lucky because many WACS during that time were not treated fairly and were ostracized for being in the military during that time. I thought it was engaging and thought provoking."—*Susan Rogers Ph.D., Colonel, U.S. Army retired.*

"In *Silence Means Security*, Barbara Nicodemus shines light into what is, for this reader at least, an unexplored corner of WWII history — the experience of young women WAC code-breakers in the South Pacific. This is more than just a history, however. Ms. Nicodemus' mother was one of those young WACs and the author's real emotional connection to her material, her desire to discover this hidden facet of her mother's life, rises to the surface on every page."—*Michael Knight, Author of The Typist, Professor of English, University of Tennessee Knoxville.*

Acknowledgment

I would like to give my gratitude and thanks to:

My husband, Randy Kurth
My brothers; Jim, Luke and Terry
The Women of Collington; Anna Shea, Sue Harpole Embree, Mary "Ricky" Evans and Mary Olmsted
My Uncle, Lloyd Nicodemus
The family of Vivian Paruta, especially Toni Baumgartner
Staci Swedeen
Barbara "Pook" Pfaffe
Ed Todd
Military Historians; Dr. David Hatch, Sharon A. Maneki, Rebecca C. Raines and Michael E. Bigelow
Britta K. Granrud (WIMSAM Foundation)
Rene S. Stein (National Cryptologic Museum)
Dr. Francoise Bonnell (U.S. Army Women's Museum)
Amanda Strickland (US Army Women's Museum)
The Staff at the National Archives, College Park MD

The only secret is the one never told! — *SIS WWII poster.*

"Women who stepped up were measured as citizens of the nation, not as women ... This was a people's war and everyone was in it." — *Franklin D. Roosevelt.*

"My best soldiers. They worked harder, complained less and were better disciplined than the men." — *General Douglas MacArthur.*

"We were sworn to silence for the rest of our lives." — *Suzanne "Sue" Harpole Embree WWII WAVE Cryptologist Naval Annex.*

x

Silence Means Security

PROLOGUE

GUARD DUTY
WHAT DID YOU DO IN THE WAR DAD
DID YOU FIGHT IN TOKYO
OR WAS IT GERMANS ON THE OTHER SIDE
THAT THEY GAVE YOU RIBBONS FOR?
NOW HUSH TALK FOR CAN'T YOU SEE
THAT I'M BUSY AS I CAN BE
IF YOU MUST KNOW GO ASK YOUR MOTHER
FOR SHE KNOWS AS MUCH AS ME
WHAT DID DAD DO IN THE WAR MOM
WAS HE BRAVE AS EVERYTHING
DID HE FIGHT THE JAPS
AND WIN THE SCRAPS
THAT GAVE US VICTORY?
NOW CHILD THERE'S SOMETHING YOU SHOULD KNOW
JUST HOW YOUR DAD FOUGHT IN THE WAR
BUT GO ASK HIM FOR YOU CAN SEE
HE'S DYING TO TAKE YOU ON HIS KNEE
WHAT DID YOU DO IN THE WAR DAD
MOM SAYS THAT I SHOULD KNOW
DID YOU WALK MANY A WEARY MILE
WITH A PACK IN DRIVEN SNOW?
MY CHILD I SEE THAT YOU MUST KNOW
IN SPITE OF ALL I SAY
I'LL TELL YOU AND YOU WILL SURELY
REMEMBER THIS DAY
NO FIGHTING DID I SEE
BUT ROUND AND ROUND I WENT
OVER A BEATEN TRACK
GUARDING YOUR MOTHER, FOR YOU SEE
YOUR MOTHER WAS A WAC
"ALABAMA"
— *PFC Ruth B. Newsome "Alabama" SIGINT WAC,*
Southwest Pacific, 1944.

When you're a child you don't always realize what they're telling you or fully understand the significance of all that is going on around you. As a girl in West Texas, I knew my mother was proud of her service in the Army. There were the framed portraits of her and my father in their military dress hanging in the hall. The occasional story would drift in and out at family gatherings. I found an album in a closet filled with photographs taken in faraway places like Brisbane Australia, Dutch New Guinea and Manila. There were images that struck me odd, like the one of women holding gas masks all in a line with those flat one story military buildings behind and another of a snow woman with her big bare breasts wearing a military cap and the words, *Miss Titts Fort Dix* written on the back.

It was the time of the Cuban Missile Crisis and I was jolted into confusion the night President Kennedy addressed my family and the nation on TV. The threat of a nuclear attack seemed eminent with the reported missile sites in Cuba. There was no discussion after his speech and the faces of my parents and brothers held no readable expression. I sensed their fear.

I awoke in the middle of the night to the sound of my brother screaming. Words, I will never forget. "Castro is after me! Castro is after me!" I stood under the door frame of my room watching my older brother franticly running up and down the long hallway that connected all our bedrooms. His eyes were wild with horror. Mama called it a night terror and said he was sound asleep.

He kept repeating the terrifying phrase, "Castro is after me! Castro is after me!" And then he was gone, darting back to his room.

The sounds of breaking glass and the thud of his large adolescent body hitting the ground made my own six-year-old body jerk. I was the first to run into his room and stood there looking down through the vacant window. He was covered in shards of glass but not much blood. He had taken the aluminum frame with him including the cross piece that helped to break his fall leaving a red mark on his forehead.

"Where am I," he said looking up at me. I knew my big brother was okay.

It would be years before I could sleep through the night alone in my own bed. During the day I was my playful gregarious self; however, at night I relived the same panic over and over I felt when my brother jumped through that window. The duck and cover drills at school, getting under our desks covering our heads with our hands and elbows didn't help. The repetitive practice to prepare us for a nuclear attack only deepened my fear.

"Everyone go back to your class."

It was November 22, 1963. I was playing Four Square on the concrete courtyard of Henderson Elementary when I heard the announcement. I remember standing there holding the rubber ball, my legs still stinging from the whirling sand devils that had convinced me to move in from the grassless playground to join the others in the popular recess game.

A strident voice blared over the loud speaker that hung above our heads. "Everyone go back to your class, President Kennedy has been shot!"

That evening, my father returned home from his delivery route. And from time to time would receive a call to pick up surplus key punch cards for recycling. He would drive a truck load of the spent cards to Fort Worth returning with money to supplement the family income. He walked through the door with a *Midland Reporter-Telegram* and plopped the paper on the red and white Formica kitchen table. The big block letters jumped out, KENNEDY ASSASSINATED.

It seemed like my mother had some kind of connection to it all. She had a bumper sticker on her car with his face on it. It read Kennedy for President. Our yard was the only one in the neighborhood with a Kennedy/Johnson sign proudly displayed at election time. Nixon signs graced the other yards. There was the photo album tucked away in the closet and the stories told when my uncles came to town with overheard words like "signal intelligence and atom bomb."

I tried to gathered bits and pieces of my mother's past life by asking her questions. Her answers were often guarded and sometimes she wouldn't answer at all. I knew it was a subject of secrets and after a while,

I stopped asking, even an eight-year-old knows not to push her mama too hard.

At first light on Veteran's Day, November 11th 2010, I laid half asleep listening to the young girl's voice inside my head realizing it was my own. "What did you do in the war, mama?"

"I worked in cryptography in the Pacific. Look in the bottom of the metal box!" she said in a Sergeant like tone, a voice I rarely remember her ever using.

I woke up abruptly and immediately went downstairs to the study. And there sitting on the top shelf of the closet was a rectangular aluminum military records box. The box my parents kept all their "important papers." The box that was always secured with a large padlock clipped to the front. The lock was there but hanging open.

I rummaged through the metal container filled with unexplained papers and there in the bottom was what she wanted me to find, military orders, letters with APO addresses and a few photos. A collection of poems typed in all caps on yellowed decaying paper were tucked in a brown envelope at the bottom.

That night she came to me again. "Tell my story, Barbara Sue." Her voice was that from my childhood, tender yet confident. "You remember what I told you. You're a smart girl. You have the letters, the orders and photographs. Fill in the gaps, make the connections."

Under much controversy, President Franklin D. Roosevelt signed the bill to establish the Women's

Army Auxiliary Corps (WAAC) on May 14th, 1942. When my mother saw her first recruiting poster of the smartly uniformed WAAC with the American Flag behind and the words "It's Your War Too," she must have thought of the motto printed above the doorway of her High School, "Enter that ye may better learn to serve."

The Japanese attack on Pearl Harbor December 7, 1941 finalized the country's commitment to World War. My mother's brothers enlisted in the Army. Dub joined the 1st Infantry bound for North Africa. Tommie joined the Army Air Corps and trained in California to serve in the Pacific.

By 1942, it was apparent that the US military effort desperately needed more personnel. Although the formalizing of military service for women occurred with the bill establishing the Women's Army Auxiliary Corps, it did not authorize equal pay, entitlements for dependents, military rank or protections under international agreements if captured while overseas. That did not happen until, July 3, 1943 when the Women's Army Corps (WAC) bill was signed into law. An effort they hoped would attract more women to serve. The Army Signal Security Agency lacked the manpower required for its highly secret cryptologic work. A huge number of recruits were needed for the tedious and copious deciphering if the highly secretive initiative would succeed. Not everyone possessed the intelligence and patience required. It was thought that women were particularly suited. A strong recruiting effort with rigid standards was established by the agency. College graduates were preferred but an IQ of 120 or higher and a score of 110 or better on the AGCT, Army General Classification Test would get you in the door to be considered for the selective positions.

The Army and Navy were looking for women with ability, integrity, discretion and loyalty to work in Signal Intelligence Service (SIS). Most of the SIS WACs were trained and stationed in the States at Arlington Hall, Vint Hill Farms and Two Rock Ranch but not all.

A few women in Special Services volunteered for overseas duty and were hand selected to get "on the job training" for the highly covert operations in Europe and the Pacific.

In the 1940s it wasn't popular for women to serve within the ranks of the military. A slander campaign fueled rumors about the "petticoat soldiers" which continued even after lies were exposed and retractions made. Rumors circulated that women were recruited into the military "to serve" the officers overseas. This was perpetuated when an article written in a nationwide syndicated column called "Capitol Stuff" claimed that WAACs were issued prophylactics before they went overseas. Others believed the rumor that a ship load of pregnant WACs were returning from North Africa. These set ideas and untruths would follow the patriotic and brave women long after their return to civilian life.

Being a female veteran made it difficult to find work after the war even for those who had acquired specialized skills. Women who served in intelligence and signal security had a double whammy, given the secrecy of the work. Recruitment statements such as, "Technical war jobs now but professional jobs later on," would seem like empty promises when hearing, "We do not hire ex-WACs."

Sworn to silence for life, most working in Signal Intelligence never shared what they did during the war, not even with their families. Sue Harpole Embree, a WAVE cryptanalyst admitted that "Even at their death beds my parents did not know what I did during the war." Why did they keep the stories hidden for so long even after the SIS records were declassified? Was it the oath taken, the vow to secrecy? Was it the prejudices that existed for WACs serving overseas? Could it be the fear of disrupting the return to "normal" and the promise of a prosperous new life in a new era?

There were over 5000 WACs serving in the Pacific during WWII. I can't help but think many of these women must have felt like my mother, who once told me, "I never felt more alive as I did back then." This is her inspired story.

San Miguel, Luzon, Philippines 1945
Luisita Sugar Plantation

"Be careful what you wish for, Billie Jean. It just might come true." She heard her mother's voice as she lay face down with M1s going off in the background.

**

"Grenade!" She dropped to the floor.

Only moments before, she was reading a teletype that had just arrived from General Headquarters. The TOP SECRET ULTRA message was now lying beside her head. Private Nicodemus grabbed the communication and shoved it in her pocket. The sound of rapid rifle fire penetrated the walls of the small hacienda serving as the SIS office. She could feel the thumping of her heart as she pressed her body as flat as possible against the wood planks.

The popping noise was relentless. Multiple shots were followed by a silence lasting only a few seconds although it seemed much longer. Every muscle of her body tensing each time the god awful racket resumed. There was nothing she could do but lie stock-still. The sound dulled as she slipped into darkness.

"Sister, get your nose out of that travel magazine and help Brother with his homework." She could see her mama's disapproving face. "Be careful what you wish for, Billie Jean. It just might come true." Mama was right, she thought. My wanderlust had gotten me into this mess but it was more than that now. I'm not the same girl I was back in West Texas. But who in the world am I? She awoke sensing an eerie stillness in the room. The only sound was the shallow breathing of her companions lying motionless on the floor. The attack had ceased as abruptly as it had begun.

***

The twenty-year-old MP knew they were out there. The coming darkness made it hard to see but he could feel it in his gut. Adrenalin rushed through his body seconds before he heard the grenade blast. He responded like a shot out of a gun. Something was moving in the bushes. He yelled out, no answer. He realized it was a Jap. Without hesitation he emptied all 8 rounds of his rifle into the dense undergrowth, pausing to reload and then to repeat. A bullet whizzed past his head as he replaced his ammo.

He turned to see the barrel of a Nambu pistol pointed at him from 50 feet away. He was sure he was a goner. Before he could respond the armed figure dropped in the tall kunai grass. "Boy that was a close one." It was Joe, his best buddy and fellow MP standing next to him poised to take another shot.

He walked over to the lifeless body in the bushes. Checking to make sure the Jap was dead, the young Corporal kicked him over and saw that the death blow was a shot to the neck. He had never killed a man before and thought when the time came he would feel more remorse. As he stood by the corpse, he was startled by the yelling, "5th Infantry 5th Infantry!" It was coming from the jungle beyond the underbrush. He recognized the Filipino accent. It was Felix. He had met Felix only days before.

The Filipino Recon unit had come into camp to make a report and get some provisions. Known as "Cat," he had gained position and status among his fellow guerillas. His uncanny ability to prowl the jungle in search of the enemy had coined him the nickname. He had proven himself time and time again a fearless hunter of men. Felix was quiet and reserved but on rare occasion would flash a wide grin reminiscent of his feline namesake. His men trusted him and would follow him anywhere. He knew they would have his back.

Felix noticed the bubbles rising up from the murky water. The reflection from the hanging vegetation made it hard to see what was underneath the greenish pool. Upon closer look he saw the tips of the straw reeds peeking above the surface. With a quick gesture of his hand, Felix signaled the other two infantrymen. They fired into the murky water.

***

"Nicky, Nicky," Billie Jean heard her military nickname being whispered with a strong sense of urgency. She turned her head realizing Alabama was trying to get her attention. "I'm going to get the gun." Alabama stood up and walked to the small table beside the bolted door. She picked up the loaded

Smith & Wesson revolver sitting in full view. Gripping it tightly with both hands, she pulled back the trigger with her thumb. Shaking, she pointed it at the bolted door.

There was a loud crash from the back of the building. The young MP had kicked in the door. He entered with his rifle in position to fire yelling, "All okay in here." Alabama stayed true to her guard. Nicky stood beside her. Other SISers moved in from the machine room. No one spoke.

There was a knock on the door. Alabama stepped back maintaining her grip on the gun. "Open the door!" Nicky recognized the voice, it was Peggy. She slowly walked to the door, flipped the bolt and opened it. Captain Margaret Turner stood meeting her eye to eye with the calmness and resolve she had always admired. Her commander entered, followed by two MPs. Peggy looked at Alabama who was still clutching the revolver. Without a word, Peggy held out her hand. Alabama gently released the trigger and gave her the gun. Captain Turner placed it back on the table.

The young MP stepped forward, "We got those Japs ma'am, all five of them, no prisoners, two behind the building. Fifth infantry got the other three back in the jungle. They were hiding under the water in the lagoon." "Just checkin' to make sure all is okay in here."

"Thanks Corporal, we'll handle it now," she said. The Corporal left the way he came apologizing about the door, saying he would get engineering to fix it right away.

Captain Turner faced her WACs. "I think you gals have had enough excitement tonight, go get some rest and report back here for your shift tomorrow. I'll stay until your replacements report." Nicky handed Peggy the crumbled teletype from her pocket. Looking down at the paper her Captain said, "I'll get this to the Major right away."

PART ONE

A West Texas Girl

Chapter I
Will I Ever Get Out Of Here?

"It sounds so far away and different. I like different places. I like any places that isn't here."
                                    -Edna Feber, Gigolo, 1922.

Saturday, March 7, 1942

Will I ever get out of Midland? Will I be stuck in this nowhere town forever? I bought a travel magazine the other day. Sure wish I could go to some of those places. Don't know if I ever will. Mama wants me to go to City Drug and see what JoAnn is up to so I'll have to keep this short. Mama's worried because of all the GIs hanging out there. Maybe I'll see Grace.

I've lost a few pounds and don't feel like a heifer. I bought a pink cashmere sweater the other day at Dunlaps and it fits me pretty good. Sure is nice to have something new to wear for a change. Much nicer than the hand knitted one Mama made for me. I like making my own money. I'm not gonna have to wash out one dress while wearing my only other like I did in high school. Wish I had some of those curlers like the beauty shops uses. Pin curls are so out of style but I have to say my hair doesn't look half bad when I smooth them curls out with my fingers. No more old fashioned hairdos for me.
Bye til later, Billie Jean

always yours Sis Jean

    Billie Jean was looking more like a woman than a girl. Tall and big boned like her father, her peaches and cream complexion and button nose gave her a look of innocence. Her gray eyes still held the same translucence as her girlhood blues. Quiet and serious, she had a sweet nature giving those who knew her well a since of comfort when in her presence.

    "Mama, I'm leaving for City Drug," Billie Jean called out as she crossed the living room towards the front door. "Jeanie, keep an eye out on your little sister and get her home early," she heard her mother say as she left the apartment. She stepped on to Baird Street and headed north to East Ohio Avenue crossing to Main. Midland was no longer just a cow town. You would see just as many Fedoras as Stetsons. Since Pearl Harbor, there were more GIs and Airmen about than oil men and cowboys, especially since the first bombardier training recruits arrived out at Sloan Field.

Lost in her thoughts, Billie Jean was unaware she had stopped at the recruiting office until she caught the eye of a handsome GI walking by. A large recruiting poster was plastered on the window. A proud WAAC in military dress was standing in front of a waving American Flag. She was wearing the signature round box hat with a disc of an imprinted eagle mounted on the front. Known as the "Hobby Hat," it was named after Oveta Cup Hobby the first director of the WAAC. The poster read, THIS IS MY WAR TOO! WOMEN'S ARMY AUXILIARY CORPS.

The image reminded her of their life in Lubbock, where being an Edwards' girl meant something. In Midland they were considered no bodies. She wanted to be like the young soldier on the poster confident with purpose and resolve. Continuing down Main her thoughts shifted to what they had written about her in the senior yearbook. She could see the words right before her as if the CATOICO lay open to the Class of 1941 page with her name and portrait.

BILLIE JEAN EDWARDS

    Moderate
    Unsophisticated
    Studies
    Is a Pal
    Chubby

The highlighted letters spelled "MUSIC" the theme chosen by the seniors that year. The annual staff thought it would be clever to use a word for each letter to describe every senior. Billie Jean didn't think it was clever but hurtful confirming what she knew they thought of her.

It was 4 o'clock on a Saturday afternoon and City Drug was jammed packed. It was where the kids hung out and the GIs came to meet girls. "Jukebox Saturday Night" was playing as she walked in the popular hangout. "Billie Jean, Billie Jean! Over here, we saved you a seat," she heard her sister's voice coming from across the room. Local girls and GIs filled small tables in the center of the room. She looked over their heads towards the soda fountain.

Jo Ann was bouncing up and down on a red and silver swivel stool waving her arms. Billie Jean made her way through the crowded store, walking past the swing dancers. She sat on the empty seat between Grace and Jo Ann. Grace was her best friend.

You would have never guess to look at them that they were sisters. Jo Ann was a beauty with long dark wavy hair. She had sultry eyes and a long neck to go with those long legs of hers. Barely 16, her womanly proportions gave the impression that she was much older. Billie Jean was nearly 18, but looked younger than her little sis. Their mama was worried, always going on about Jo Ann staying out late with boys. Billie Jean kept telling her, "They're not boys, Mama."

Jo Ann Edwards Age 16

Behind the counter was a Soda Jerk dressed in a white shirt and bow tie tapping cokes from a gooseneck spout. A short order cook was standing at a grill. They ordered hamburgers and cokes. GIs kept coming up to Jo Ann. One asked her to dance to Gene Autry's "Be Honest with Me." Others offered to pay for their food and drinks. Billie Jean tried to discourage their approaches by saying she had it covered but you could tell that Jo Ann loved the attention. When it appeared that Jo Ann was getting a little too friendly with her dance partner, Billie Jean walked up to her and said. "I promised Mama you would be home early."

"Just a little longer," Jo Ann said. She remembered what happen last Saturday night when she came in after midnight. Helen, their oldest sister, was home for the weekend visiting from Big Springs. All hell broke loose when Jo Ann walked through the door. Helen got all worked up and called Jo Ann "trash." The whole thing ended with Jo Ann and their mama crying.

***

September 5, 1939

I met the neatest gal today in shorthand class. Her name is Grace. We hit it off right away. She's a little bit of a thing, barely over five foot tall. Struck up a conversation with me right away. Said she loves sports and typing. I've seen her before in the grassless field beside her house playing ball with her brothers. At the time I thought what a spunky girl, she can really take it from those boys. She's all smiles but there's something sad about those eyes of hers.

Grace said she was excited about learning shorthand. Me too. We have two business classes together. I bet we're going to be great friends.

Billie Jean

Billie Jean and Grace

July 14, 1940

    Grace wants me to run away with her. She said she's been saving her baby sitting money and we can take the bus to San Angelo. I've been saving my baby sitting money too. Thought I might buy a typewriter. Hire myself out like Mr. Miller suggested. I know Grace is unhappy. Her home life is bad with all that fighting and drinking going on. I don't think she should go away by herself. Beside we're best friends.
    I hate to see her quit school but she seems determined to leave. We only have one year left. She's a dynamo at shorthand and could get a really good job if she would

finish. Maybe I'll go and try to talk her in to coming back. It's over 100 degrees and dry as a bone. Hearsay its cooler and greener in San Angelo. There's a river and lots more trees.

   Billie Jean

July 20, 1940

   We took the bus to San Angelo. Not much cooler here than back home. However, after riding in that hot bus for 5 hours sure did feel nice sitting under those trees. It's a pretty town with the Concho River running right through it. There's a park next to the river with lots of cottonwoods and oaks.
   Grace said she had a cousin that might put us up but we couldn't find her. We looked in the phonebook and asked around town but no luck. We found a cheap motel not too far from the park. I was afraid the motel clerk would ask us what we were doing in town but he didn't when he saw we had cash money to pay. Grace keeps saying we could get jobs and find a better place to stay. I told her I was going back. I don't have any reason to run away from home. I know mama's worried. Grace is stubborn. She's not coming back with me.

   Billie Jean

July 27, 1940

   Grace came back yesterday. Sure was glad to see her. She wouldn't tell me what happened to make her change her mind. Don't matter if she doesn't want to tell me. I'm just happy she's back and we can finish school together. Grace said she's going to knock the top off her business classes so she can get a stenography job with one of the oil companies after graduation. I don't know what I'm going to do, get a job too I guess. Wish I could go away to college but given the way things are no chance of that. You have to come from money to go to college.

Billie Jean

***

Not a cloud in the sky, another sunny day at Midland Army Flying School. More clear flying days than any other place in the nation, ideal for the new bombardier school. The outstretched Permian Basin was the remnants of a vast inland sea that existed over 250 million years ago. The flat land with endless sky was ruled for hundreds of years by the Comanche until the Indian polices of the Texas Republic eliminated the threat. Piles of buffalo bones, remnants from the white buffalo hunters could still be found on the desert wasteland surrounding the base. Countless "Jackass" rabbits, scorpions, rattlesnakes and prairie dogs inhabit what was once shared with free roaming cattle.

An Army weather station had been set up on the private airfield in the late 1920s. With the war ramping up in Europe, it was natural that the Army would consider Sloan Field for an air school especially with local business men and political heavy weights pushing the issue up in Washington. By July of 1941, it was a done deal. The field was leased to the U. S. Government for a dollar a year.

Not long after Pearl Harbor, plans changed for the small flying school located between Midland and Odessa. With the invention of the revolutionary Norden bombsight, the Army decided to designate the airfield as a bombardier school. They were gearing up with the intention of making it the largest bombardier training facility in the entire country. Hundreds of military personnel were arriving every week in support of the effort including Medical Supply Sergeant Donald L. Nicodemus.

Nick stepped out of the Infirmary. He wanted to make sure the supplies that arrived the day before had been put in order before he went into town. He walked down to the post office where Wayne was waiting outside in his 1928 Model A Coupe. When he got in the car, Wayne said, "God-forsaken place, not a tree in sight, found a god damn rattlesnake in my barracks last night. Wish I was back in Muskogee closer to home. I hear that the gals in Midland are wide-eyed and purrty."

Wayne worked in supplies, been on base a little over a week. Nick met him when picking up his special issue shoes to accommodate his short wide feet. Wayne was a wiry 23-year-old Corporal from Oklahoma, friendly as all get out and he had a car.

Nick and Wayne walked into the City Drug Store, "Take the A Train" was playing. Nick had always liked Duke Ellington although Glen Miller was his favorite. He would check the juke box later to see if they had "In the Mood". He immediately spotted Billie

Jean and Grace sitting at the soda fountain. Nudging Wayne he looked in their direction.

Sgt. Donald Lee Nicodemus Age 26

With Nick in the lead, they headed straight for the girls. "Hi, I'm Nick and this is Wayne. Can we buy you ladies a soda?"

***

Morning of March 8, 1942

JoAnn woke me up this morning jabbing her finger in my shoulder. "You were with a GI last night. Tell me all about it," she said. I hate getting up early when I don't have to. She went on and on. I finally told her to get out and that it was none of her business.

    Diary, I will tell you all about it. I did meet a GI last night. His name is Nick. He's a Sergeant, handsome, not very tall maybe an inch taller than me, but he has broad shoulders and the most striking blue eyes. I first noticed his eyes from across the room. His uniform was starched with his shirt perfectly tucked and his blond hair was peeking out from under his cap. He has a kind face. He walked up to Grace and me with his buddy Wayne and asked us if he could buy us a soda, I think he meant coke because when Grace nodded straight away he ordered 3 coca colas and a cup of coffee for himself. He's from somewhere up North, I could tell from the way he talked. Wayne sounded like an Okie. "Take the A Train" was playing on the jukebox and Nick said he had seen Duke Ellington play once in Chicago. He was so forward, no one has ever come up to me like that before.

    After we finished our cokes, he asked if we wanted to go for a ride and see the sunset. Grace was game but I wasn't so sure. But I agreed, he was cute and kept looking at me with those blue eyes of his. When I first saw Wayne's car, I thought what an old beat up jalopy but on closer look I saw that it was a Model A with a rumble seat. I had never ridden in a rumble seat before. It was tricky getting in but Nick took my hand and showed me how. I stepped on the bumper and then the fender grabbing a handhold to pull myself in. Nick jumped right in after me. We drove out the Andrews Highway and pulled off on the side of the road at the edge of town.

The sun was low and the sky was streaked with peach and yellow lighting up the prairie. It changed so fast. The robin's egg blue behind the clouds got darker and flickers of orange shot straight up and then the sun disappeared. I've seen hundreds of sunsets on the prairie but none like that. Stars popped out in all directions. There must have been a million.

Wayne broke out a flask. Grace took a sip right away. She handed it back to Nick and he asked me if I wanted some but I said no. Then he took a big swig. He asked me again before taking another. I was relieved when he handed the flask back to Wayne.

A cold breeze stirred up and I started shivering. Nick asked me if I was cold but didn't wait for me to answer. He put his arm around my shoulder pulling me close. Then he grabbed one of those green wool army blankets from the floor board and pulled it up around us. He told me how nice my sweater felt, looked me in the eyes and kissed me. I've never been kissed like that before or that long. He's going to pick me up next Friday night at six and take me out for a steak dinner.

Billie Jean

***

March 13, 1942

Bad luck comes on Friday the 13th or that's what Mama says. My date with Nick didn't go well. Mama's always spouting off some old wise tale or superstition, don't ever borrow salt, don't walk under a ladder, break a mirror and it will bring you seven years bad luck. I don't believe in those old Irish superstitions of hers, but all I know is our date started off fine and ended in a disaster.

 Nick drove up in Wayne's car without Wayne. He came inside and I introduced him to Mama. He was polite took his hat off and told her it was nice to meet her. Mama brought us some sun tea. Nick said he had never had sun tea before and it was the best tea he had ever drank. He had a nice conversation with Mama. She asked him where he was from. He said South Bend, Indiana and that he had two sisters and a bunch of brothers. He told her he had joined the Army in '38 and liked being stationed in Midland where everyone was so friendly.

 He took me to Big Ed's Steakhouse on Wall Street. It was much nicer than Big Ed's old place. It had long picnic tables covered with red and white gingham table clothes. I reckon a steakhouse is a more fitting establishment for a new sheriff than a sandwich shop. The place was filled with servicemen and their dates. I noticed a couple of girls from school but they paid me no nevermind. We ordered T-bones and baked potatoes. The waitress brought out a carousel with all the fixins. I put everything on mine. Nick only put butter and bacon on his.

 When the waitress took our plates, Nick said there was no reason to hang around Midland because he knew a place out on Highway 80 towards Odessa where we could get a drink. And then he did the funniest thing, he placed his finger in the air shaking it to indicate he wanted the check.

 That was the first time I've ever set foot in Honky Tonk. No Honky Tonks in Midland, it's dry. I heard some of the supper clubs are serving beer since the Army Air Corps is in town. No one makes a big deal of it, its wartime and it means lots more business. I wish we had gone to one of those supper clubs. This place stunk to high heavens and was dark and smoky. There were women in tight fitting dresses milling around. Nick ordered bourbon on the rocks with a splash of water. I ordered a coke.

One of those women, the one in the snug low cut red dress came up to the table and stood next to Nick. When he didn't pay her any attention, she sat right down in his lap. She looked at me and said, "Nick, what are you doing with such a baby when you can be with a woman." When I stared at Nick, he pushed her off and picked up his glass. I told him to take me home. He threw back his drink and we left.

I didn't say good bye when he dropped me off. I just got out of the car and walked straight to the apartment. I was so embarrassed. I will never let anything like that happen to me again.

Billie Jean

March 23, 1942

I don't know why but I agreed to go to the movies with Nick. He kept on calling and calling. Finally, I decided to talk to him. He invited me to a double feature at the Yucca on Saturday. He said he was really sorry and asked me to give him another chance. I told him I would go to the matinee and meet him there.

The Yucca is my favorite theater. It's the most exotic building in Midland. The first movie I saw there was The Wizard of Oz. I love the song that Judy Garland sings,

"Somewhere over the Rainbow." I wonder why I can't fly beyond a rainbow like the bluebirds.
  Billie Jean

***

Billie Jean saw Nick standing between the sandstone and black marble columns under the red and white striped awning. She noticed that Nick looked a little nervous, almost boyish with his hand in his pocket jingling his change. Nick had arrived an hour early to get the tickets. Good that he did for shortly after, a long line formed around the gothic style twelve-story Petroleum Office building next to the Yucca. As he waited for Jean, he had plenty of time to look at the tall impressive buildings that made up downtown Midland.

He didn't recognize her at first. Her hair was pulled back and she had on red lipstick. She was wearing a dress that showed off her figure instead of the skirt and baggy sweater she had worn before. He took his hand out of his pocket. "You look very pretty," he said as he took her arm to go inside.

They walked past the ticket booth and through the gilded foyer to the concessions, where Nick bought Jean some popcorn and a coke. They stepped inside the theatre with its two tiered balcony and elaborate light fixtures. The stage and movie screen were draped with a thick velvet curtain. The only reminder that you were in West Texas was the golden cows jutting out from a top of the two scrolled columns, one on each side. They decided to sit downstairs four rows back and to the left across from the large bearded wood carved Sphinx.

March 26, 1942

I enjoyed my afternoon with Nick. I love going to the movies especially at the Yucca. We didn't talk much at first. This was Nick's first time in the Yucca. He was looking all around, I could tell he liked it. He said it reminded him of the stories his Grandma Nick use to tell him, stories of kings and riches in the desert from the Bible. We sat in the theater and admired the golden lions painted halfway up the walls. To me those cats have always seemed like they are walking around the room protecting me from the outside world.

We saw a light hearted western comedy called Valley of the Sun with Lucille Ball and James Craig and an animated Walt Disney motion picture called Fantasia. There was an intermission between the two so we went outside for a smoke. Nick told me he liked my hair. When I smiled at him he said he was sorry about the other night. I told him it was best not to talk about that. I didn't want to stir things back up and spoil my mood for Fantasia. Maybe it was the dancing hippos or the magical Mickey set to symphony music, but Fantasia put us both in a good humor.

After the movie, we went to a new place that serves up frozen custard from a machine. It was delicious. They sell it out of a window down on Main Street. We waited in line for thirty minutes to get some. Boy was it worth it.

Nick couldn't stop talking. He told me all about being a medical supply Sergeant. He wants to go overseas but not in the medical corps. They turned him down for flexible gunnery school, said he was too old and that the Army needs experienced supply Sergeants over here. So he's trying to get in a petroleum unit because he thinks that's his best chance to get to Europe.

Out of the blue he asked me, what I wanted to do. He caught me off guard and I blurted out that I wanted to get out of Midland and see the world. That's the first time I've ever said it out loud. I can't believe how easily it slipped out and that Nick was the person I told.

Billie Jean

Chapter II
BILLIE JEAN

Won't you come over to my house
Won't you come over to play
I've got lots of plaything, a dolly or two
And I live in the house cross the way
I'll give you candy and sweet things
I'll put your hair in a curl
Won't you come over to my house
And play that you're my little girl
       —Lullaby sung to Billie Jean

Christmas Day 1935

 Daddy dropped over dead yesterday morning. He was in a hotel room in Seagraves. Bad heart they say. We were all waiting for him. He promised he'd be home Christmas Eve to help us kids put up the tree. We just kept waiting. Finally, Helen told us to start decorating the tree. A policeman came up on the front porch asking for Mama.
 Everyone was there but Ruth. Helen and her new husband, Fred came all the way from Big Springs. Ruth's in Roby with her Ma. I don't really know my half-sister. I've only seen her a couple of times when Daddy brought her by the house. Tommie lives with us. Moved from Roby a few years back. Boy does Tommie and Dub get along you would think they were blood brothers instead of step

brothers. I remember them talking up that they were gonna hop a train to California come spring. That kinda talk made Daddy mad.

I keep thinking about Mama. She's seen some misery in her life. Losing her first born because of those coal embers jumping the fire on to the baby's blanket. Her first husband, Helen and Dub's dad died of a heart attack just like Daddy. Her second husband got shot on a train. And then there was the time our house burned to the ground when I was a little girl. I remember holding mama's hand watching it burn.

When the policeman came to tell Mama about Daddy, we all went out on the big porch. The kids too, Katie, Junie, JoAnn, Jimmy and me. Jimmy's only seven and now he's gonna have to grow up without a daddy. We haven't even opened our presents, everyone is so sad.

Billie Jean

Bascom Johnson Edwards, known as BJ, was a wheeler dealer and they say he could sell a glass of water to a drowning man. In fact, that's how Nancy Emmaline Hall met the dashing salesman. It was 1915 and he was working in a Wichita Falls' music store. He saw the handsome widow through the display window admiring a beautiful oak upright Lester piano. BJ sold her that piano and won her heart. Emmaline didn't need a new piano but couldn't resist his charm.

The Edwards family came to Texas in the early 1870s from Tennessee. Silas, BJ's dad, worked the family farm in Comanche County until he met and married Celina Hogan. The family farmed in Callahan

County for a few years and then moved to Fisher County to settle in the community of Roby. Silas and Celina weren't much for the farming life and settled on the hotel business. They owned a couple of hotels while BJ was growing up with his brothers and sisters there in Fisher County.

BJ made money fast, lost it just as fast. He was always selling something, pianos, cars, real estate. He even tried his hand at wildcatting. Not long before he died, he'd sunk all his money and then some in to an oil and gas deal, prospects in Gaines and Yoakum Counties. At the time of his death, BJ and his partner were still on the outs because of the affair.

Bascom Johnston Edwards, 1935

Helen had an affair with his partner. BJ adored Helen even though she was Emmaline's daughter from her first marriage. Only eight years old when they married, she quickly warmed up to her new daddy. Cute as a button, the petite sassy lass won his heart. Maybe it was because he had left his own daughter back in Roby with her mother or because she was always climbing in to his lap vying for his attention. Helen was in her mid-twenties at the time of the affair. She was a lively young woman, loved to dance and go to the honky tonks. Five foot two, she wore her hair in a bob. On Saturday nights, she'd get all dolled up, put on her short dress with the wrap around fringe and go out dancing.

This affair tore BJ up. He felt Helen was faultless even though she was old enough to know better to get involved with a married man. It ruined the friendship and put a strain on the partnership. The oil and gas deal was sealed with a handshake right before BJ found out. In the oil patch, a man's word and handshake was considered a binding agreement. The Bank transferred the money and no legal papers were drawn up between 'em.

January 20, 1936

We had to bury Daddy in the pauper's cemetery. Mama said we didn't have the money to bury him in a proper grave. It was cold and snowing when we put him in the ground. Mama said that the bank was going to come take our house. There's no money for Katie to stay in college either. Mama's hoping we can stay in the house until school is out. There's talk of moving to Big Springs come summer.

Mama's always playing those sad Irish tunes on her piano. Sometimes she gets her mouth harp out and plays a jig to try and lift our spirits. The same tunes her grandpa and uncles use to play on their fiddles back in Alabama. Dub and Tommie are talking about hopping a train to California again just as soon as the weather clears. They say they want to get out before the dust and heat comes back. No work for them around here anyways. I feel like everything is falling apart. Sure do miss my daddy.

Billie Jean

***

Emma June and Billie Jean were only 14 months apart. By the time Billie Jean was three, she was the same size as Junie. Their mama dressed them alike and people thought they were twins but they couldn't have been more different. Junie liked to play in the dirt and Jeanie with dolls. Junie like to climb trees and Jeanie play school. Katherine Lena was seven years older than Billie Jean, always bossing her sisters around like a second mother. They knew their big sister loved them but it was hard to tell. She treated those cats of hers better than her kin. Katherine did have her favorite. When Billie Jean got gravely ill, it terrified her at the thought that she might lose her baby Sis.

Emma June, Katherine Lena and Billie Jean

The strangling angel of death almost took Billie Jean's life. She was three turning four when she contracted diphtheria. BJ had an experimental serum flown in from Dallas. The doctor injected her the night she almost died. She was so sick with fever they feared she would not last till morning. The Methodist minister from their church contacted a faith healer named Edgar Cayce in Virginia to pray over her that night. The illness stripped her of her voice and she did not speak for nearly two years. "Don't worry about

Billie Jean, she's quiet as a church mouse," they would say.

Billie Jean could read the worry all over their faces. She chose not to speak. Every time she tried fear built up inside. She remembered the pain and swelling in her throat cutting off her life's breathe.

By her sixth birthday she had begun to talk again but remained painfully shy. Billie Jean was excited about going to a real school even through her pensive nature didn't show it. Katie liked to play teacher with her and Junie. Junie often ran off to play outside with the boys leaving Billie Jean as her only student. Katie taught her the alphabet and how to write her name.

It was the end of the school year. Everyone was expected to read aloud to the class. One by one her classmates walked up to the chalk board, faced the rows of seats and read. Her heart raced each time a boy or girl finished their passage. Her anxiety building as each student reclaimed their chair. Finally her time came. "Billie Jean it's your turn," declared Miss Jackson. When she didn't respond, she said, "Billie Jean everyone else has read to the class except you. You must come up right now and read." She slowly got up and walked to the front of the class. When she turned around and saw her classmates, she froze. "Go ahead," her teacher said. She looked down at the page knowing every word but couldn't speak. She dropped the open primer right in place, didn't even hear it hit the floor. She ran through the open door all the way home.

Her mama listened patiently while she told her what had happened. Taking her by the hand, they silently walked back to school. The warmth of her hand and calmness of her touch made Billie Jean feel that everything would be okay. Her mother led her back to her desk and she sat down. She kissed her forehead and then left. No one made her read aloud that day but she did find the courage the following week. Billie Jean began to flourish with her new found courage. She would even raise her hand on occasion to go up to the board to demonstrate multiplication tables.

Her underlining fear subsided, only to come back with an incident she was not prepared for. It happened when she was only nine. The children were working at their desks, practicing their cursive writing when she felt a moistness between her legs and a slight cramping down low. She stood up noticing there was blood on her chair. The back of her skirt soaked. The fear rose up inside the same as it had when Miss Jackson demanded she read in front of the class. She felt the blood run down her inner thigh and thought something was terribly wrong.

Billie Jean ran out the open classroom door towards home like she had three years before. Rounding the corner of her street, she could see her mama hanging out laundry. "Mama, I'm dying!" she yelled.

Jimmy was born at home. She remembered feeling his kicks in her mama's swollen belly. So when her mama told her she would bleed every month and that her body was preparing for when she would became a full grown woman, she acted like she understood. Helen and Katie confirmed the reason for the assault with stories of their own but she had more questions than answers. Why hasn't this happened to Junie, she's older? And what did bleeding have to do with baby making? The next summer she found her mama's medical book hidden in a drawer. She looked at the pictures and read about how babies were made. She thought she would have none of that besides Katie had warned her about boys.

September 1, 1935

School starts next week and I have two brand new pairs of shoes thanks to Daddy. He drove me all the way to Dallas to one of those fancy downtown shoe stores. You know the ones that specialize in hard to fit sizes. I was wearing the toes out of my loafers and Daddy said, "Sister, we can't be having you in shoes that don't fit, ruin your feet. I'll have to take you to Dallas and get you some uptown shoes." I jumped two sizes in half a year. The man who measured my feet said I was a size nine and that my feet were as thin as pencils.

We drove all the way to Dallas in Daddy's new Oldsmobile stopping the night in Abilene at a motel on the side of the road. We stayed in a real swanky place in Dallas, just me and him. There was dark wood on the walls. Daddy said it was wall nut. A wall made of nuts? It looked like wood to me.

We got all dressed up for dinner, Daddy in his best suit and me in my Sunday dress, the blue one with the gathered skirt. I tied my hair up with a light blue ribbon and wore my new black patent leather shoes.

The dining room was beautiful. All the tables had white table cloths with china plates so shiny you could see your face in them. A waitress came up to our table and called my daddy by name like she knew him. I think she was overly friendly. She asked about me. Daddy told her my name and said I was pretty as a picture and smart as a whip. She looked at me and asked if all his girls had those eyes. He said, crystal blue just like their mama's. Then she said something about Dallas going wet and asked my daddy if he waited a whiskey. When she brought him that whiskey, she touched him on the arm. I didn't like the way she touched him but Daddy didn't seem to mind.

Billie Jean

Chapter III
Winds of Change

"Yesterday, December 7, 1941 — a date which will live in infamy"
— *Franklin Delano Roosevelt.*

June 10, 1936

Mama tried to keep us together but with Dub and Tommie hopping that train for California and Helen and Fred in Big Springs, everything has gone to hell in a hand cart. They came and got Daddy's Oldsmobile. Too bad for Katie, she had just gotten her license to drive it. The last straw was when the bank took our house. Even with Katie getting a job to help out Mama couldn't make the payments. Mama sold everything except for Daddy's Philco Cathedral radio. She even sold her piano.

We rode the bus all the way to Big Springs. Helen and Fred took us in. It's so cramped here, all of us living in this tiny two bedroom house. But not for long. Katie got a job in Midland working for a Lawyer. She found us an apartment downtown and we're going to move there next week.

Billie Jean

May 28, 1937

It's my thirteenth birthday. We had the same dinner as usual, beans and cornbread. Helen made me a cake. It was a yellow cake with cream icing. There wasn't a crumb left. Katie gave me a Ladies Home Journal magazine. Now that I'm thirteen I can start babysitting. Help out like Katie. Things have been rough lately. I heard Mama and Katie talking. We're behind on the rent and we might have to move. Katie got mad and said, we're not that destitute that we have to live on the wrong side of the tracks! It's hard on Katie trying to provide for all six of us.
   Billie Jean

June 15, 1937

We must be the poorest white family in Midland if mama has to clean houses. There may be a depression going on but in Midland there's still people with money. Oil, cattle and cotton rules around here. And Mama is cleaning their houses. She doesn't seem to mind. She says things will look up now and we can stay put.
   Billie Jean

***

June 1, 1940

Junie got married. She dropped out of school to marry Junior. Mama and Katie didn't like that Junie dropped out but seeing they were so much in love and had their minds made up, wasn't much they could do. The Bizzells are cotton farmers. Junior's daddy gave them a piece of land a *couple of miles out of town toward Stanton. Junie didn't like school much anyways. We've been in the same grade since she was put back. I sure will miss her next year. Junie will love living on a farm with all those animals. She's a hard worker and will make a good cotton farmer's wife.*

Katie met someone too. His name is Bill Savage. They met in Big Springs while she was visiting Helen and Fred. He seems nice, kinda quiet, and easy going. That should be helpful in getting along with Katherine. He's got a good job as a welder. They go out every weekend. I've never seen Katie so happy.

Billie Jean

Jimmy played on the Midland Junior High Football Squad Billie Jean's senior year. He was a big boy and excelled in the sport. He had no problem blocking those farm boys and rancher's sons creating a spot for himself on the Bulldogs the following year. His sisters were not surprised how quickly he made first string. Jimmy became a star athlete and academic scholar. He was determined and highly motivated. "Football is my ticket to College," he would say. "I'm going to be a lawyer someday." Katherine planted that seed in his head. Billie Jean noticed how easily he made friends even with the wealthy kids. Football would be his ticket.

October 30, 1940

Katie and Bill got hitched today. They went over to Big Springs and got married by a Justice of the Peace. Bill got

a job down in Galveston at the shipyard. They're leaving tomorrow, said they'll have their honeymoon down there at the beach. He's gotta start work on Monday. Katie told mama not to worry she would send money every month like clockwork. I don't see Junie much since she moved out on the farm and now Katie is going to be so far away. I have my school work to keep me busy.
    Billie Jean

May 29, 1941

    I graduated today. I walked across the stage like everyone else thanks to Katie. She sent me the money for my diploma, cap and gown. I got a job keeping books for the Walker-Smith Wholesale Grocery Company and start on Monday. I'm going to make $22 a week! First thing I'm going to buy is a portable Royal Typewriter. They said I can buy it on time, five dollars a week and in eight weeks it will be mine, free and clear. I bet I can make another $5 a week picking up typing. I want to buy one of those Pendleton bath robes and get my hair fixed in a beauty parlor. Of course, I'll give money to Mama every week so she won't have to clean houses.
    Billie Jean

***

Jimmy walked over to the Cathedral radio and turned it on. They always tuned in to *The Jack Benny Show* after Sunday supper. "President Roosevelt said in a statement today, the Japanese have attacked Pearl Harbor Hawaii from the air." blared the NBC news bulletin.

"Jeanie, Jeanie. The Japanese have attacked Hawaii!" yelled her little brother.

Billie Jean almost dropped the plate she was drying. She managed to place it on the counter before joining the others. Jimmy, Jo Ann and her mama were huddled in front of the radio. *"We will interrupt all programs to give you latest news bulletins. Stay tuned to this station."* The orchestra opened the program with "A Gay Ranchero" leading in to a JELL-O commercial.

No-one could concentrate on the banter between Don, the show's announcer, and Jack. Their voices blew past them like tumble weeds in a blowing sand storm. They were listening to Dennis Day sing "Everything I Love" when he was abruptly interrupted.

"Ladies and gentlemen, a special announcement. The entire regular personnel of the sheriff and police office has been placed on a two-platoon basis with twelve hour shifts. All auxiliary personnel have been directed to stand by for emergency service instructions. The regular county defense program is functioning in an orderly manner, and citizens are urged to remain calm and avoid all unnecessary confusion because of hysteria. Citizen volunteers are asked to go quietly to their nearest police or fire stations and offer their services if they wish to help. There is no immediate cause for alarm, and coolness will accomplish more than anything else."

"Boy they must be going crazy out there in California," said Jimmy.

The following day everything stopped mid-day. Not a soul was on the streets of Midland. It was like a ghost town. Everyone was inside listening to President Roosevelt's radio address to the nation including Billie Jean and her co-workers.

> "Yesterday, December 7, 1941 a date which will live in infamy, the United States of America was suddenly and deliberately attacked by naval and air forces of the Empire of Japan.
>
> The United States was at peace with that nation and, at the solicitation of Japan, was still in conversation with the government and its emperor looking toward the maintenance of peace in the Pacific.
>
> Indeed, one hour after Japanese air squadrons had commenced bombing in Oahu, the Japanese ambassador to the United States and his colleagues delivered to the Secretary of State a formal reply to a recent American message. While this reply stated that it seemed useless to continue the existing diplomatic negotiations, it contained no threat or hint of war or armed attack.
>
> It will be recorded that the distance of Hawaii from Japan makes it obvious that the attack was deliberately planned many days or even weeks ago. During the intervening time, the Japanese government has deliberately sought to deceive the United States by false statements and expressions of hope for continued peace.
>
> The attack yesterday on the Hawaiian Islands has caused severe damage to American naval and

military forces. Very many American lives have been lost. In addition, American ships have been reported torpedoed on the high seas between San Francisco and Honolulu.

Yesterday, the Japanese government also launched an attack against Malaya.

Last night, Japanese forces attacked Hong Kong.

Last night, Japanese forces attacked Guam.

Last night, Japanese forces attacked the Philippine Islands.

Last night, the Japanese attacked Wake Island.

This morning, the Japanese attacked Midway Island.

Japan has, therefore, undertaken a surprise offensive extending throughout the Pacific area. The facts of yesterday speak for themselves. The people of the United States have already formed their opinions and well understand the implications to the very life and safety of our nation.

As commander in chief of the Army and Navy, I have directed that all measures be taken for our defense.

Always will we remember the character of the onslaught against us.

No matter how long it may take us to overcome this premeditated invasion, the American people in their righteous might will win through to absolute victory.

I believe I interpret the will of the Congress and of the people when I assert that we will not only defend ourselves to the uttermost, but will make very certain that this form of treachery shall never endanger us again.

Hostilities exist. There is no blinking at the fact that our people, our territory and our interests are in grave danger.

With confidence in our armed forces — with the unbounding determination of our people — we will gain the inevitable triumph — so help us God.

I ask that the Congress declare that since the unprovoked and dastardly attack by Japan on Sunday, Dec. 7, a state of war has existed between the United States and the Japanese empire."

December 11, 1941

We are now at war with Germany and Japan. Dub called and said he's coming home to Texas to enlist in the Army. Tommie's going to stay in California and try to get in the Army Air Corps out there. I walked pasted the Recruiting Office today, most of the boys I know from school were in line. Everyone's enlisting.

President Roosevelt said, "December 7, 1941 a date that will live in infamy." I know I will never forget that day. The day Pearl Harbor was bombed. The day the United States of America was attacked.

There was a wind storm today. The sand blew and the wind howled. I think everything is gonna change.
Billie Jean

Chapter IV
Donald Lee

"This is not the first time I have visited the site of this great dam. And it gives me extraordinary pleasure to see the great dream I have long held taking form in stone and cement. This dam is the greatest engineering work of its character ever attempted at the hand of man"
—*President Herbert Hoover, November 12, 1932*

The boys were crouched down in a half circle huddled at the end of the alley. You could easily identify the Nicodemus brothers by their straight blond hair and their dominance among the other boys. Thirteen-year-old Don was the shooter. His brothers Paul and John were cheering him on. He loved shooting dice and seemed to have the touch. Shaking the dice in his right hand, he gave them a quick blow before letting them go. His brothers always placed their bets on Donald. He rarely lost on the come out roll.

The dice forcibly hit the wall bouncing on the ground finding their place to an easy way eight. "Come on Big Eight," Don said in a strong voice, as he picked up the dice for another roll. Rolling a hardway would make him a lot more dough if he could get the others to raise their bets. Don was feeling lucky so he asked if anyone would double their wagers on a hardway. He had a couple of takers. Letting go of the dice, he repeated the mantra, "Come on Big Eight the hardway." The gutsy bet had paid off, lying there on the ground were the desired two fours.

Donald Lee was born February 9, 1916 in Peru, Indiana to Lydia Mae Osborne and Deo Brant Nicodemus, the sixth of nine children. Lydia was only fourteen when she married the twenty-two-year-old Brant in 1906. Nine children in fifteen years may have taken a toile on the overly sensitive young women. When Donald was eight years old his mother left the family. He chose never to see her again.

Don liked running free in South Bend with his brothers, swimming in the river, playing craps on the street, smoking and drinking forbidden liquor in the back alleys. He hated going home to the small cramped drafty wood frame house his father had built to bring the family from KoKomo to South Bend. He didn't get along with his step mother.

Lena had married his dad a year after his mother had left. Brant had a good job on the line at the Studebaker auto factory and Lena was recently widowed with five children. By the time they moved to South Bend in 1926, there were twelve children living at home with one on the way. Lena and Brant liked to play cards and drink on the weekends, leaving the older kids to take care of the younger ones. Often there was not enough food in the house for all those growing boys so the older Nicodemus boys learned to fend for themselves.

***

On a crisp autumn afternoon in 1934, the Tip Top, a small watering hole in Kellogg, Idaho was crammed packed. Ray Morgan the proprietor and newly hired eighteen-year-old Nick from South Bend, Indiana were hustling behind the bar drawing drafts and pouring bourbon. The Tip Top was popular with the Bunker Hill miners but on this particular Saturday night a few miners from Wallace were out in search of a change of scenery and cheaper drinks. The Sunshine Mine had just struck a bonanza silver vein and with all the celebrating in Wallace, the bars were crowded with liquor going for a premium.

For the most part the Bunker Hill and Sunshine miners got along fine but the later it got and the more alcohol consumed the more it started to get out of hand. One of the Sunshine miners blurted out, "I don't believe that god damn story about grubstaking Noah Kellogg and his Jack Ass finding his lode." Every one of the Bunker Hill miners stood up and surrounded the accuser. "Let's take him out back," said the biggest of the bunch. Before you could count to three, Nick came out from behind the bar and stood between the two factions. "Time for you guys to be getting back to Wallace," he said. "Beers all around," Ray yelled from across the bar. The three out-of-towners ducked out the back door. Ray knew then and there he had found a keeper in the young man from Indiana.

***

Silver Valley sure is a fine place. Never thought I'd be back here. The green mountains of Idaho was sure a relief after riding for days in that box car across the plains. Cecil and I jumped off to get a bath and something to eat at Depot Hill in Kellogg. The people were friendly and didn't seem to mind that we were passing through.

Cecil left home at sixteen when Dad moved us to South Bend. I was ten. He said he couldn't take it anymore living in that house. Cecil held on to his kitchen job until the Depression closed the diner. He had it in his mind that we could get jobs working on the Boulder Dam and talked me in to going with him.

The road heading to the gate was littered with empty liquor bottles. Broken glass everywhere. Boulder City was a Company town built from the desert up. Bone dry so to speak, no liquor allowed. I saw a guy guzzle his down. The tossed bottle crashing on top of the others. A fence was put up at the railroad pass to keep those who didn't belong out. Only those who had papers for jobs or relatives living in Boulder City were allowed on the reservation. The fence didn't keep men from trying.

We waited in a long line for hours to reach the gate. When we got to the check point, there were a couple of company men asking questions. The man asked me my age. "Too young," he said. "Dangerous work. We're looking for men with skills." "You got any work experience?" The man asked looking at Cecil. Cecil told him he had worked in kitchens. "Anderson Brothers looking for dishwashers at the mess hall. You mind washing dishes?" He had to take it. We were near broke.

Cecil handed me his last five spot and said, "You get back on that train and go home." I stayed the night at the squatter's camp, a half mile or so away. Boy was it a hell hole. Beat up tents and lentos scattered about. Hundreds of men lying around. I met a couple of guys from Indiana, turned down same as me. They gave me some of their campfire beans cooked in a can.

There was talk in the camp about mining work in Northern Idaho which got me thinking about Kellogg. I didn't want to go back home. I had a job as a rum runner, running liquor from South Bend to Chicago but that all dried up with the end of prohibition. Dad moved the family on a small farm after the house burn down. The family was larger than ever. I couldn't see me doing farm work and playing second fiddle to all of Lena's kids.

***

He hopped off the train at the Depot and noticed the Tip Top right away. He decided to go in for beer and fish around. It was three in the afternoon and the saloon was near empty. Don sat at the end of the oak bar and ordered a beer. The middle aged bartender asked what brought him to town. He noticed the *Bartender Wanted* sign located behind the bar. "I'm looking for work," he said. "Did a little bartending in South Bend." He stretched the truth a bit. He had bartended a couple of times at a speakeasy and had a familiarity with the business from the time he ran liquor. Ray, the bartender liked him straight away. "What's your name, son?" "Nick."

***

Another hard mountain winter was around the corner. Nick felt restless and homesick. He missed his brothers and his sis, Hazel. He decided to give her a call. She said that Art had joined the Navy and Cecil the Army. "They'll be looking for good caddies back at the Coquillar Golf Club and Paul says you're a shoe in. You could play the amateur circuit with him this spring." "What are you doing way out there? Come home Donald," she told her little brother. "It would be great to see you for Christmas."

Nick liked working at the Tip Top and Ray paid him a respectable bartender's salary of $35 a week. But he longed for the trappings of the city and the winters here were even colder than South Bend. *I don't know what I'm looking for but I know it's not here in Kellogg.* This time he bought a ticket to ride the train.

In the early spring, he took a bus to Peru to see his Grandma Nicodemus. She had moved in with the family when his mother ran off. After Brant and Lena got married, she went back to the home place. Walking down the familiar dirt road, he thought about how much he missed the tough old bird. You always knew where you stood with her. She wouldn't put up with no drinking or cursing. Didn't go hungry when she was around, Grandma always made sure there was plenty to eat.

When he approached her house, she was sitting in a rocker on the front porch all bundled up smoking a corn cob pipe with her bible in her lap. "Donald my boy," she said as she gave him one of her big bear hugs. The next time he saw her, she was laid out in a casket.

The Nicodemus family at Grandma Nick's funeral. Left to Right – Art, Cecil, Betty, Paul, Deo Brant, Lloyd, Donald, Hazel, John, Ray

Paul was the better golfer but Don could sure give him a run for his money. He was fourteen when Paul got him on as a caddy at the Coquillar Golf Club. In

1937, they both played in the Indiana Amateur Golf Tournament. Don beat his big brother by 3 strokes.

Caddy wages weren't much so Nick tried to enlist in the Army. They turned him down twice. But he kept on trying thinking his odds would get better. Right before Christmas, he got a letter to report for basic training after the first of the year.

***

May 9, 1942

Nick drove up in a black two door Chevy sedan this afternoon. He'd made a good deal and wanted to show it off. It's a 1936 model. It was so shiny, he must have been waxing it for hours. We drove all over town. Even went up Hwy 349 past Midland Country Club. We stopped at the end of the golf course and he mentioned that he missed playing golf with his brother Paul.

Nick knows all about my family but I know almost nothing about his. I thought it was a good opportunity to ask him some questions. He's never mentioned anything about his folks. But when I asked him about his mama, he got real upset. After a long pause, he said his mama was a loose woman and that she ran off and took baby Lloyd with her. They found them in a hole-in-the-wall motel. The baby was so bad off they had to take him to a hospital. "The baby was near dead."

I thought he was going to cry. The muscles in his face tightened and he became flushed. His feelings seemed all twisted up. I didn't know if he was sad, angry or deeply hurt. He looked so vulnerable. I tried to change the subject but he just got dead silent.

Billie Jean

May 28, 1942

It's my eighteen birthday! Nick took me to the Ranch House. It's the nicest and most expensive restaurant in town. He came to pick me up early but I wasn't ready so he had to wait. He looked so handsome leaning against his car in his dress uniform and hat in his hand. His hair was neatly parted in the middle. He's a good looking guy. I ordered some ankle trapped shoes from Dallas and got a new dress to wear.

At dinner Nick gave me a gold heart necklace. I was so surprised when I opened the black felt box. It's 24 carat gold! He moved around to the back of my chair and fastened it around my neck. It lays perfectly above the V neckline of my dress. I think Nick was trying to make up for pressuring me the other night to go to bed with him. He said we could go to Big Springs and get a room. I let him know then and there I was not that kind of a girl. I would have to be married to do that.

Nick was very sweet tonight. I've never seen him so sweet. He took my hand and looked me in the eyes and said, after this war he'd get stationed in Europe and take me with him. He said we ought to get married.

Billie Jean

Chapter V
Summer 1942

White Sands
Somewhere in the heart of North America there is a desert where the heat of several suns has fused the particles of sand into a single sheet of glass so dazzling it sends a constant signal to the moon.
  —*Marianne Wiggins, Evidence of Things Unseen*

The smell of Helen's peach cobbler filled the house, the aroma seeping through the back screen door. Bowls of pinto beans and a plate piled high with her sweet corn bread lay on the kitchen table for the taking. The temperature had already reached above ninety on this early Sunday afternoon, the first day of summer. A jar of sun tea rested on the back porch step. Freddie Don was playing in the dirt with his toy trucks. Under the lone cottonwood tree was a piece of plywood setting on two saw horses covered with a floral bed sheet. Mismatched side chairs surrounded the makeshift table.

The family was gathered at Helen and Fred's for a good bye supper. Bill had gotten Fred a good paying job at the shipyard in Beaumont. They would be leaving in less than a week. June and Junior arrived with Jimmie Dale who was dressed in miniature western wear. Junie had made the shirt for her adorable eight month old out of a printed flour sack. His child sized cowboy hat swallowed his head covering his eyes. Delma Ray, Junior's younger brother came in behind.

Delma Ray was fun loving, always joking around. He was a charmer with his good looks, thick wavy hair and easy going smile. At sixteen, he was too young to enlist but he kept sayin' that as soon as they would take him he was going to join the Army.

"Hey Nick!" Nick looked up. Fred tossed him a beer. Catching it with one hand, he grabbed the church key off the table and opened it. "Never had a *Pearl* before." Junior and Delma Ray reached in the cooler and took two cold ones. "Come on and get some beans and cornbread before they get cold," Helen yelled out from the backdoor. Everyone got their grub and found a place at the open-air table.

It had been months since they had all gotten together. The conversation was lively. "We'll be walking in high cotton come soon," said Junior. His cotton yield looked extremely good. With the war going on and the increase demand, he would get his best price ever. Jean was relieved she was working full time as a stenographer so she wouldn't have to be a picker. The last time she picked cotton her fingers bled and her back hurt for weeks. Fred said he would have a victory garden down in Beaumont. "You can grow anything down there. Lots of rain and rich soil."

"Don't have to worry about those horned killer jack rabbits down in Southeast Texas," Delma Ray said, thinking Nick might take the bait. Nick had been around long enough to know of the hoax of leaving strangers out in the desert to look for the mythical critter. So, he just laughed with the others. Jean noticed how comfortable he'd become with the family but he hadn't met Katherine yet. When Katie found out that Jeanie was dating a 26-year-old GI, she called home right away. "You've got to break if off," she told their mama. She was fuming when she talked to her little sis. "Jeannie what are you thinking, he's too old for you and you know he's only after one thing."

June 21, 1942

Helen, Fred and Freddie Don are moving to Beaumont. Bill got Fred a job at the shipyard where they're building battleships. Katie says she can get me a good job down there. I have mixed feelings about going. Sure would like to see Katie's new house. She sent a photograph. It has a front porch and a high gable. It's painted white with yellow shutters and is on a real nice street with a boulevard. Katie's doing her part working as a riveter. Bill started calling her "Rosie" like in the song which makes her mad as a hornet. Katherine never could take a tease.

I guess Katie will have to stop working soon. She's expecting her second. I'm still mad at her. She keeps writing mama and telling her to forbid me from seeing Nick. I'm eighteen and can see who ever I want. Besides Katie has her own family now and needs to keep her nose out of my business. Mama hasn't said a thing to me but I found the letters. I think Mama likes Nick but I know what Katie thinks does matter to her. Everyone else in the family seems to like him. You should have seen how they were all joking around today.

After supper, Junie asked me to do the dishes with her. I think she wanted to get me alone to ask about Nick. She said that it looked like things were moving pretty fast. I didn't know what to tell her. She said she could tell he was in love by the way he looked at me. I do have feelings for him. He doesn't treat me like a nobody. Everyone is moving on with their lives except for me.

Billie Jean

***

June 27, 1942

Nick asked me to marry him last night. He wants to elope. He said it was tricky getting leave because of the Big Air Raid show planned on the 4th of July. He'll pick me up at dawn on Friday and we'll get married in Big Springs at the courthouse. He gave me an engagement ring. He bought it at the Post Exchange. It has a real pretty little diamond. I'll need to hide it real good so JoAnn doesn't find it and spill the beans.

Billie Jean

***

The Bombardier College had erected a model of Tokyo 17 miles south of the flying school for the staged demonstration. The "Hell from Heaven Men" and their 75 twin motored bombers would drop their eggs methodically on the miniature Japanese capital while an estimated crowd of over 10,000 spectators watched in aah. It was expected everyone on base would attend.

Nick had different plans. He was way over due for leave and had worked diligently to get all the medical supplies in order before the aid raid show. He asked off for the same weekend to get married convincing his CO to pull strings to make it happen.

***

Night had set in by the time they arrived at the Hotel. Nick signed the register Mr. and Mrs. D. L. Nicodemus. He insisted on their best room. Jean stood by his side in her wrinkled cotton suit feeling dusty, hot and exhausted from the long drive. Jean thought about calling home but realized it was too late. Nick went out to find something for them to drink while Jean took a bath.

When he returned, he noticed she had pulled the blackout curtains. It took a few moments for his eyes to adjust, the only light coming from a brass floor lamp in the corner of the room. She was standing in front of him, the lines of her body transparent through the gauzy robe. He placed the whiskey, small bucket of ice and bottle of lemonade on the bedside table. He told her he wished it was Champagne but this was all he could find besides beer. He mixed her a whiskey and lemonade in a hotel water glass. He poured himself a straight whiskey. She asked him for a cigarette and slightly shook as he lit it. They slowly sipped their drinks.

Nick placed his empty glass down. He asked her to stand and untied her robe letting it drop to the floor revealing a form fitting satin gown underneath. Without a word, he pulled her down on the bed.

***

She woke up consumed with thoughts of how worried her mama would be with her absence. When she first tried the party line, it was busy. "Jean?" "Yes, mama it's me. Nick and I got married yesterday in Big Springs."

There was a pause and then her mama spoke. "I just got off the phone with Junie and she said that she wouldn't be surprised if you got hitched." Jean interrupted saying, "Nick's on leave and wanted to drive out to White Sands. We're staying at the Alamogordo Hotel. We'll be home late Sunday night."

They drove down US 70 towards the National Monument. The entire highway was covered with white sand. You could hardly see the road. Nick focused on the barely visible yellow line down the center. Jean noticed an occasional yucca roadside. There appeared to be mountains in the distance but he couldn't discern how far. As the wind picked up, the sand blew around the car coating the windshield. It stuck to the glass like refined table sugar, easily swiped away by the windshield wipers.

Billie Jean had visited the park before with her sophomore science class. She heard lectures on how the gypsum sand had washed into the Tularosa Basin from the surrounding San Andres and Sacramento Mountains for thousands of years. Nowhere to go, it deposited over time forming the enormous dunes with the help of the unremitting winds.

They checked in at the entrance taking the Dune Drive into the park. The vast white sand stretched out as far as the eye could see. Nick had never seen anything like it. When the wind subsided, they got out of the car and started walking on the glistening gypsum under the noon day sun. The expansive beauty was awe-inspiring. Jean noticed a desert lizard race between them, white like a ghost.

Unbeknownst to them, they had just crossed a route that the Spanish conquerors called Jornado de Muerto or the Journey of Death. They managed to walk to the top of a large dune and sat down facing north. The newly formed Alamogordo Bombing and Gunnery Range lay just 25 miles way.

Of course, they didn't know that in two short years they would have had the perfect vantage point to witness the secretive "Trinity" detonation and the huge mushroom shaped cloud that would loom over head.

Chapter VI
The War Hits Home

Are you a girl with a Star-Spangled heart?"
— *1943 WAC Recruiting Poster*

November 1, 1942

    Nick tried to get us Off-Base housing but was turned down. There's so much activity at the bombardier school they want him to stay on base. We found mama the cutest house to rent on North Colorado just blocks from my office. It's a white wood framed shot gun with a small front porch and a fenced backyard. Jimmy's always wanted a dog, maybe he can get one now. The house is much bigger than the apartment. Jimmy and I have our own rooms. Nick spends the night when he can. Jo Ann's not happy about having to bunk with mama.
    Billie Jean

December 25, 1942

    Katherine and Little Billy came home Christmas Eve. We were all excited. Mama was the only one who's ever seen Little Billy. She took the bus all the way down to Galveston when he was born. He was so cute toddling in through the front door in his sailor suit. Having a little one around sure does lift mama's spirits. Everyone gets so down in the mouth this time of year ever since Daddy died.

Katie and Nick got in to it. Katie kept glaring at him. He was just sitting in the living room when she let in to him. I heard her say, "If you ever hurt my little sister, I'll kill you and I mean it." Mama and I were making pies when Nick walked in and left through the back door. Katie kept going on and on about me getting married so young, ruining my life.

I didn't know if he would come back but he did. I was taking the last of the pies out of the oven when he came home. Everyone else had gone to bed. He stumbled through the door, drunk as a skunk. When I saw the puppy in his arms, I kept my mouth shut. We kept the precious mutt in our room until Christmas morning. You should have seen the look on Jimmy's face when he saw that pup. Everyone was on their best behavior on Christmas, even Katherine.

Billie Jean

***

Jo Ann met Luke Griffin Gallagher, a new bombardier recruit at a honky tonk in February around her seventeenth birthday. He was a good dancer and she fell head over heels for him. The love affair lasted about six weeks. Luke finished his instruction and got a commission as a 2nd Lieutenant in the Army Air Force and immediately left Midland for a new assignment. He promised her he would be back to see her.

Nick applied for flexible gunnery school. For the second time they turned him down, telling him that 27 was too old, and they needed experienced supply

Sergeants stateside. He sent another request for a transfer to the Fuels and Lubricants Division. Medical supplies was getting him nowhere. He thought transferring to the ever expanding Quartermaster petroleum unit would get him the experience he needed to go overseas.

Nick got orders to report to Ardmore. The Oklahoma Army Air Field was expanding to accommodate the Second Air Force, Bomber Command. B-17 aircrews would be put through a grueling and rigorous training to expedite their readiness for combat overseas. The Fuel and Lubricant unit was increasing personnel to meet the needs of the 24-hour training schedule. Nick jumped at the chance. There was only one problem. Jean wouldn't be able to go and would have to stay in Midland.

***

Billie Jean answered the door. The color went out of her face when she saw the Western Union man. "I have a telegram for Mrs. B. J. Edwards from the US Army." She reached out and he handed it to her. It read, THE ARMY MINISTRY REGRETS TO INFORM YOU THAT YOUR SON PRIVATE WILLIAM L LEWIS IS MISSING IN ACTION. LETTER TO FOLLOW.

"Who was that?" asked her mama. She knew when she looked in her daughter's eyes and saw the telegram in her hand that her worst fear had come true. Dub, her eldest son, was dead or missing in action in North Africa.

May 14, 1943

The Axis Powers surrendered in Tunisia yesterday and we haven't heard anything about Dub. No letter or nothing. Ever since Nick left for Ardmore, Katherine's been badgering me to come to Beaumont. Maybe I'll go. Katie's pregnant again, expecting early September. Bet she can use some help besides she says I can get a civil service job with the Navy and do my part. Not much happening around here except waiting for that letter. Nick wants me to stay here. He says I'd be closer when he gets leave. Mama's so worried about Dub, she don't say much. I've got lots to think about.
    Billie Jean

June 3, 1943

Dub's alive! Mama got a letter from the Army. He's in a military hospital. His Commanding Officer wrote the letter and said they found him buried in the sand. He's not out of the woods yet and he could be in the hospital for two more months. We're all hopeful that he'll pull through and be home soon.
    Billie Jean

Dub had been fighting for over a week in the Western Desert. The Germans were holding strong. Dub and his best pal were side by side when the blast hit and a wave of sand tumbled over them. He would lie beside his dead friend for days in the desert of North Africa before they found him.

August 8, 1943

> *I quit my job. I'm leaving tomorrow for Beaumont. Nick hasn't been home since he left and doesn't think he'll get any leave anytime soon. Mama wants me to go since Katie is due in 3 weeks. After her miscarriage, she got pregnant again right away. She says she needs to stay in Midland and keep an eye on JoAnn and Jimmy. I'm excited about going. I've never been to the coast. I've always wanted to see the ocean. I guess the Gulf of Mexico will have to do.*
> *Billie Jean*

***

The Army Recruiter noticed the tall young women approaching his desk. She was neatly dressed in a straight skirt and pullover sweater with her hair pulled back. He had placed the new WAC poster in the window the day before. It read, *Are you a girl with a Star-Spangled heart?* JOIN THE WAC NOW! THOUSANDS OF ARMY JOBS NEED FILLING!

He hoped it would draw someone in. The young well-groomed Sergeant with the winning smile extended his hand to her. As they shook hands, he said, "Sergeant Reynolds at your service, ma'am. How may I help you?"

"I'm interested in what kind of jobs the Army needs filling."

"Are you from around here?"

"I'm staying with my sister and her husband. They work at the shipyard."

"And your name?"

"Billie Jean Nicodemus"

"Well, Billie, we are looking for bright women 21 to 45 with no dependents who want to serve. Do you have any clerical skills?"

"I worked as a bookkeeper and stenographer back in Midland."

"Children?"

Shaking her head she indicated no.

"We're looking for women just like you to train for technical war jobs which will mean professional jobs later on. All I need is your birth certificate, a willingness to serve and I can sign you up."

"I'm not 21, turned 20 back in May. I don't have my birth certificate either," she told the recruiter. The lie slipped out without much thought. The sergeant flashed her a confident smile and said all she needed was two close relatives to come in and sign an affidavit swearing her age. He didn't see a problem given her birthday was back in May. "The Army generally makes allowances for exceptional applicants like you."

Billie Jean did have a problem. She was only nineteen and how was she going to convince her sisters to lie about her age and sign the paper?

November 2, 1943

I can't believe Katie and Helen didn't put up a fuss about signing the paper. I think having a baby girl has softened Katie at least for the time being. She's been pushing me to go to work at the shipyard but I have bigger ideas. Sergeant Reynolds said the Army was looking for WACs for Special Services. I don't know what that means exactly but he said if I did well on my IQ test and the Army's general ability test, I would be a shoe in.

I called Nick to tell him I enlisted and he said he wasn't surprised. All is going fine in his petroleum unit but he doesn't think it will be his ticket overseas. There is so much training going on at Ardmore it's even hard to get any leave. It's been 7 months since we've been together and I'll be off to basic training soon. I'm leaving for Houston tomorrow to be sworn in, catching the 8 a.m. bus.

Billie Jean

On November 3, 1943 Billie Jean Nicodemus officially enlisted in the Women's Army Corps. The next afternoon, she boarded a train for Fort Oglethorpe, Georgia.

PART TWO

"You're In the Army Now"

Chapter VII
Heart and Soul

Duty is calling you and me
We have a date with destiny
Ready, our hearts are ready
Our pulses steady,
The world to set free!
Win it! We're in it heart and soul
Victory will be our only goal
We love our country's honor
And we'll defend it against every foe!
—*WAC Lyrics to Colonel Bogey, British Army Marching Tune*

She looked out the window into the pitch black. The clickity clack and rocking of the rails serenaded her like a mother's lullaby. Sleep would evade her however, for as soon as she fell asleep the steam whistle would blow. Most of the travel was at night moving across the Deep South. Billie Jean was hoping to get a glimpse of Alabama, the birth place of her mother, Nancy Emmaline Hall.

It was too dark to see anything. Her mother had come to the Lone Star State as a young girl in a covered wagon and told stories about her grandfather, William Alexander Hall's loyalty to the South.

Grandpa "Pone" had lost two brothers in the war, one at Gettysburg, the other in a prisoner of war camp at Harpers Ferry. Against the advice of his older brothers, he joined the Confederate Army as a drummer boy and was there at Gettysburg when his brother was killed.

Grandpa Pone was a fine musician and played the fiddle. He taught Emmaline how to play the mouth harp. She was close to her grandpa until she married her first husband. He was a Yankee. Her grandpa would never forgive her. "No Damn Yankee is ever gonna set foot in my house as long as I'm alive, just let him try. I'll shoot the son of a bitch."

The train approached Chattanooga at sunrise, winding through the ridges and valleys. A fog lay across the bluish mountains with the sun peeking through. Most of the trees were bare, a few left with a smattering of yellow and red leaves hanging on. An occasional cluster of evergreens glistened from the early morning dew.

A city bus was waiting at the Chattanooga station to take the recruits the eight miles to Fort Oglethorpe, Georgia. Billie Jean patiently hung back to witness the assortment of young women. The mixture of southern drawls, monotone mid-western talk and the rapid banter of big city gals excited her.

They were dropped off at the Reception Center on the South Post. The 3rd WAC Training Center was located south of the well-established Post of Fort

Oglethorpe on federal land which had been the Chickamauga Battlefield during the Civil War.

The Post had a colorful history occupied by the Cavalry for decades. During World War I, it was a major mobilization center for the Army as well as the site of the largest German prisoner of war camp in the country. By World War II, the post was a large Armed Forces induction center. Male and female military were segregated with WACs assigned to the South Post.

***

We were poked and prodded in all directions. I hate shots. They scare me to death. After I got sick, BJ made sure all his kids got the Diphtheria vaccine. I was there in the hospital when Junie got hers. She grabbed the big needle and put it on her lip. She let out a scream. Junie has a scar on her lip that will never go away.

We're sleepin' on cots in an old WWI barracks. We use outhouses called latrines and have to shower in outside wash houses. They say we'll be here until we get assigned to a Platoon. I hear the WACs barracks on the South Post are much better.

They sent us to the supply warehouse for uniforms, underwear and shoes. The underwear was the same olive drab OD color as our wool uniforms. Don't know why they gave us winter uniforms. It's warm and humid down here. My skirt is too short, my jacket too tight and my shoes too small. The coveralls they gave me ride up in all directions. Nothing fits except for the Hobby hat.

Day one, they marched us. And we've been marching every morning since. My toes and heels are raw. My feet swollen. I can barely fit my feet in my boots. The only relief I get is during the lectures and testing in the afternoons.

They tested our IQs and gave use the AGCT, Army General Certification Test. We were issued a training manual called *You Must Be Fit* and told to read it. There in bold letters it said, **Your Job: To Replace Men. Be Ready To Take Over.** It's a how to book, how to exercise, how to have good posture, how to have good hygiene, how to march, how to swim. I sure hope we don't have to swim. There's even a section on the Army Way to health and added attractiveness, skin care, make-up and hair styles. I guess there's an Army Way for everything.

I met Lieutenant Reed our Company's supply officer on my second visit to get additional gear from the warehouse. Lieutenant Reed was a great gal. She greeted everyone with a warm smile and boy is she efficient. When I told her that my shoes hurt my feet, she went out of her way to find me better fittin' ones. She asked me my size and when I said nine and a half, she looked in my shoe and said, they had given me eights. She disappeared behind the shelves and came out with size nine boots and shoes. I'm grateful for the Lieutenant's special attention. She told me she hoped the boots wouldn't rub blisters on the ends of my toes during our long marches but nines were the largest they could issue.

Lt. Reed, Fort Oglethorpe, GA 1943

As I turned to leave, Lieutenant Reed called out, "Nicodemus, don't forget your collar pins." She handed me the US mounted metal disc and another disc a little larger than a quarter with the raised head of a helmeted goddess. "Wear those with pride," she said. "The Pallas Athena is our insignia, issued only to the WACs." I loved studying mythology in school. Athena was my favorite goddess. She was smart and courageous. I thought what a fitting symbol for the

Women's Army Corps, Athena the goddess of reason and mercy in war.

We were waiting in line to be issued our fatigues when I heard a laugh. I turned around and found the cheery recruit two rows over fluffing the curls in her blondish hair with her fingers. Our eyes met and she flashed me a smile. As I walked out of the supply warehouse with my gear in my arms, she bumped my shoulder. "What's your Company?" she asked.

"Company 11," I replied.

"Agnes Bard, you can call me Corky. Got that nickname because I'm lively. What's your name?"

"Billie Jean Nicodemus."

"With that accent you must be from somewhere like Texas."

Corky, looked down at the papers in my hand and said, "I'm from Buffalo. Well Nicky, looks like we're in the same Platoon. I know we're going to be the best of friends."

Thank goodness she didn't call me something like Tex. Nicky, I can live with. A new Mess Hall and Recreation Building occupied the center of the South Post. Double rows of one story white barracks were on either side. I was pleased to see indoor toilets and showers instead of outdoor latrines and wash houses. Bunk beds filled the room. The bunks were arranged in perfectly straight lines only 3 feet apart. A footlocker was placed at the end and to the side of each bunk. Long clothing rods hung against the walls.

Sheets, an OD wool blanket and a pillow were on each bed.

"I'll show you only once," said the Corporal. "All racks will have hospital corners." She demonstrated the 45 degree fold.

If our Platoon Sergeant told us once she told us 1000 times. "There's the right way, the wrong way and the army way. I'm here to teach you the Army Way!" Katie would have made a good Platoon Sergeant.

We were trained how to eat, how to shower, how to brush our teeth, how to dress, how to wear our hair, even how to walk. "Only one way to walk as a WAC, head up, back straight, buttocks in and remember to suck in that tummy!"

We were up and at 'em at 0500 with lights out at 2100. We marched every morning after breakfast and most afternoons. We marched in the sun, in the rain, in the sleet and in the mud. Even our personal time was scheduled, one hour each evening in our barracks right before lights out.

Living in a large group of women don't bother me much. I guess having all those sisters prepared me for waitin' my turn. Showering bare naked with all the others took some getting use to. All the women in my Platoon have graduated high school and many have gone to college. It's a sharp bunch of gals and we get along just fine. We're all here for the same reason, to serve our country.

***

Nicky told Corky she'd lied about her age to get in the service and that she was only nineteen. Didn't take long for Nicky's secret to circulate around. Not even the Platoon Sergeant cared that she was underage. Nicky was more than capable and showed abilities well above the average WAC recruit. They liked to tease her about being the baby of the unit. Her even-temper and quiet way made her an easy target for pranks.

Nicky was getting up to return her tray when the Corporal ordered, "Nicodemus, it's regulation, you must eat the entire skin of your baked potato, no waste in the Army." Nicky looked down at her tray. She had never eaten the skin before. She sat down and began to cut it in to pieces. She actually liked the earthy taste. When she finished, she noticed a couple of recruits laughing.

Nicky always ate the skin of her baked potato after that. When asked why, she would say, "Because I like it." Five weeks down, one to go and Billie Jean and Agnes hadn't gotten their assignments.

"Nicodemus, Bard, the Major wants to see you. Report to her office at 0900," said the Corporal during morning inspection. Both had scored high on their IQ and AGCT tests. Their abilities as skilled typists were confirmed. Nicky knocked the top off the dictation test. Now it was the Major's decision where to send them.

Finally their orders came. They were elated! They would both be going to Fort Dix. Nicky would serve under Major Frank G. Hartleroad the Commanding Officer of Special Services. Corky received a general assignment to report to 2nd Service Command. Corky was especially overjoyed. "Nicky, we will be stationed at the backdoor of New York City! You'll love New York. Dancing, theatre, fashion, Champaign and men!"

***

It was graduation day and as they marched, a military brass band played in the distance. They rounded the corner entering the park circle. The central parade ground was surrounded by turn of the century houses. Officers and enlisted men stood at attention on the large porches. The bleachers were filled with WACs. The music was coming from a white gazebo bandstand perched at the end of a large grassy area. Their voices rose as they moved closer with the heartfelt lyrics coming to life.

> "We're in it heart and soul
> Victory will be our only goal
> We love our country's honor
> And we'll defend it against every foe"

They were soldiers now. It was not just a man's war. And as they advanced, they felt they were marching to their destiny, none more than Billie Jean.

On December 23rd, Nicky left Fort Oglethorpe for Fort Dix.

Chapter VIII
Live for Today
Fort Dix, New Jersey, 1944

The train pulled in to Fort Dix, New Jersey on December 24th. Billie Jean arrived not knowing a soul. Corky had gotten leave to go home for the holidays. Nicky was eager to start her first assignment as a stenographer in Special Services but there was the familiar feeling that always washed over her every Christmas Eve. She felt a deep sadness. She felt alone. On Christmas Day, she called home and wrote a letter to Nick.

In less than 24 hours she would be reporting to her first official duty. She missed Corky but didn't know when she might see her again. She hoped they'd be assigned to the same quarters but given Corky was in a different outfit was not expecting it.

It was the day after New Year's and the other WACs would be returning anytime. She sat on her bunk in the empty barrack's thinking about what to write Katie. She would ask her to send a crossword puzzle book in her next package. Before she could put pen to paper, she was interrupted by a recognizable laugh coming from outside. Corky burst through the door with someone Jean thought looked familiar but couldn't place.

Corky plopped on the rack next to Jean. "Hey Nicky, look who I bumped in to. Do you remember Vivian from Fort Ogle?"

Jean smiled at the petite dark haired WAC. Corky and Vivian had been sworn in together at Grand Central Station. Their WAC Company was the first from New York. They arrived for basic together but were put into different platoons. Little did they know that the three of them would become the best of pals and would see each other off and on until the end of the war.

It was a cold and snowy January at Fort Dix. Nicky and Corky were more than ready for their first three-day pass. They knew exactly where they would spend it, New York City!

There were crowds of service men and women getting off trains at Grand Central Station on that sunny but cold Friday afternoon. Rays of light were streaming down from the upper arched windows of the Grand Hall. It was more spectacular than the image she'd seen in *Look* Magazine. The rumble of the voices heightened her expectations. *I'm in the Big Apple.*

They immediately headed to the Commodore Hotel. It was close by and Corky had gotten the scoop of special rates for military. The porter insisted on taking their bags to their room. The man at the reception desk asked if they had dinner reservations and suggested the 21 Club on West 52nd. He made them an eight o'clock reservation and ordered them a cab. "I can't believe how helpful everyone is," Nicky told Corky. Back home their always sayin' New Yorkers are cold as fish and stand offish." Corky explained to her the custom of tipping.

***

Twenty-one cast iron Jockeys were lined up on the balcony standing guard. They wore different colored waist jackets and white knickers. We walked through wrought iron gates to get inside the club. Red and white checkered cloths draped the round tables. Big Ed's has the same table cloths on his picnic tables but this room looks classier especially with the beautiful wooden bar at the back. I felt under dressed until I noticed more than half the room was filled with service men and women in uniform.

"Good evening ladies. There's some gentlemen over there who want to buy you drinks," said the waiter pointing to the Sergeants sitting a couple of tables over. One caught my eye, a broad shouldered guy with thick brown wavy hair. He noticed I was looking at him. He gave me a wave. I noticed his large hand and long fingers.

"What should we order?" I asked Corky.

"Manhattans of course."

Lifting our cocktail glasses, we looked in their direction, smiled and mouthed thank you. Corky said, "Let's invite them over?" She gave them a wave.

Before you knew it they were sitting at our table. The red haired freckled faced one took the seat next to Corky. The tall good-looking one pulled a chair close to me. Sean, the Irish looking one, said he was from New York, the Bronx and that his Pop and uncles were firemen. "Firefighting is in our blood. When this war is over, I'll join Engine 43 Company," he said.

Jack sat next to me. He worked as a carpenter in Pennsylvania before joining the Army. We hit it off right away. Jack asked me all kinds of questions about Texas, said he had always wanted to see those wide open spaces. "It's true what they say about the girls from Texas."

"What's that?"

"Prettiest you'll ever see." His comment made me blush. "Hey you gals want to go dancing tomorrow night at The Stork Club?" Jack asked.

***

"I'm not going dancing in this OD uniform. Let's go to Bloomingdales," Corky said. "Maybe, we can get our hair done?" said Nicky.

Neither one could sleep a wink that night. Both were wound up tight as a drum from the excitement of the evening. They stayed up talking, making plans for the next day, lunch in Central Park and then off to Bloomingdales.

Jack and Sean waited at the door of the popular dance club as the girls got out of the cab. They moved quickly and took their arms to walk inside.

Jack removed Jean's wrap and gave it to the hat check girl. She's a knockout, he thought. The skirt of her navy blue chiffon dress fell right below her knees and he noticed her long legs and sheer stockings through the side slits. Jean looked very put together. Her make-up, applied perfectly, accenting her cheekbones. Her up do with a pompadour on top gave her an air of class and sophistication.

Corky looked great too. Her green taffeta dress, synched at the waist with full skirt screamed let's dance. As soon as they got seated at the café table, Sean grabbed Corky's hand and pulled her out to the floor for a swing dance.

While Corky and Sean danced, Jean and Jack talked. They stopped their conversation only for the occasional slow dance. When he put his arm around her waist, lifting her ever so slightly against his torso, her heart raced. She felt like she would drop to the floor if he let her go. She intuitively followed his every step as he guided her across the dance floor.

It was lightly snowing by the time the guys took them back to the hotel. Sean and Corky went in to the lobby but Jean and Jack remained outside. The cold snowflakes falling on her face made her shiver. She tightened her wrap. Her senses seemed heightened. She could see and feel his breath. She knew what she wanted. She wanted him to kiss her.

"You're cold," he said placing his arms around her shoulders. Jack pulled her close and they kissed. "Jean, I want to see you again."

Corky and Billie Jean woke up at noon. They had matinee tickets for their last day of leave to see Rogers and Hammerstein's *Oklahoma!* The USO at Fort Dix had given them the coveted on Broadway tickets.

The marble, stone & stucco façade of the St. James Theatre stretched along West Forty-Fourth Street. They walked through the spacious marble lobby into the auditorium with decorated mural side walls and proscenium arch. They took their floor seats a few rows back from the stage. "Boy these are great seats," said Corky. The curtain parted with a cappella opening number, "*Oh What a Beautiful Mornin*" sung by the handsome cowboy Curly McLain.

Billie Jean had never felt so happy.

***

The poster hung on the Mess Hall wall, white crosses marking graves with the words, *Women! They can't do any more — but you can*. It was a daily reminder of the sacrifice. Sons, husbands, fathers, brothers lost.

Nicky was staring at the poster when Corky shoved the advertisement in front of her. "Let's write an essay for this contest," she said. The Canadian Women Army Corps and the WAC Second Service Command came up with the essay contest as a goodwill gesture between the Corps. Two Canadian WACs would be wined and dined in New York City and two U.S. WACs would be given the royal treatment in Montreal. The women who were declared to have the best answers to the question, "Why the WAC Needs You?" would be the winners.

Corky, Vivian and Nicky, Fort Dix NJ 1944

Vivian, Corky and Nicky, all had brothers in the Army. It was expected that their brothers would join up or be drafted. Corky sparked something in Vivian when she brought up the subject. Quiet Vivian could hardly contain herself. "I always felt it was unfair that my brothers were not required to help around the apartment. It's a matter of fairness! When they were drafted I felt that if they had to do it, then I had to do it too. Besides, I know that God will take better care of us if we were all in it together. When I heard the rumors about the women in the Auxiliary Corps, it made me want to join even more. My family still doesn't understand."

Jean's motivation to do something worthwhile drove her just as hard as her desire to get out of West Texas. She was not the kind of girl who would be satisfied waiting for something to happen or waiting for her man to come home.

Unable to get a teaching position in Paterson, New Jersey after graduating college, Vivian unhappily took a clerical job in New York City. The despair she witnessed in her Italian neighborhood day to day especially after Mussolini brought Italy into the war was unbearable. Corky was restless and teaching English at the local high school didn't fill the void. Both wanted to do more.

"*U.S. WACs Holiday in Canada, Two contest winners date, dance, ski on a flying trip across the border,*" read the *Look Magazine* article. Pat Davis, 25, ex-Chicago sportswear buyer and Agnes Bard, 22, ex-Buffalo school teacher had won the essay contest. Pat and Corky both felt the high point of the trip was the time they spent at Laurentain Mountains Lodge. Their Austrian ski instructor was surprised at how easily the two newcomers picked up cross country skiing. He believed the Americans learned easily because they were accustomed to exercise and responded readily to discipline

Corky came back exhausted from the four-day world wind. "I slept the whole way back on the plane," she told everyone. "We were greeted by the Mayor of Montreal and the Canadian military entertained us to the max. We danced on the roof of the Mt. Royal Hotel! Our escorts were so cute. One of the Sergeants even wore a kilt." Jean was impressed with how Corky went after what she wanted and made it happen, like winning this contest. She clipped out the article, folded it and put it in her pocket to save as a keepsake. Billie Jean would find herself reading it again and again especially when her confidence got low.

On the roof of Montreal's Mt. Royal Hotel, Pvt. Pat Davis dances with kilt-clad Sgt. James Downey, Black Watch, Royal Highland Regiment, who has been in uniform since 1933.

U. S. WACs Holiday in Canada
Two contest winners date, dance, ski on a flying trip across the border

Pat Davis, 25, ex-Chicago sportswear buyer, has been a WAC eight months; Agnes Bard, 22, ex-Buffalo school teacher, is a rookie of ten weeks. Because both had strong reasons for joining the Army, because both were able to put their ideas down on paper clearly, they were the two winners in a Second Service Command essay contest on "Why the WAC Needs You."

Prize was a four-day vacation as guests of their Canadian counterparts, the CWACs, who had already held a similar contest, with a trip to New York as the reward. Object: partly a holiday for the girls, partly a good-will gesture.

Although Pat lost ten pounds during the trip —"I was having too much fun to eat"—and Agnes slept through nearly the whole plane trip home, the vacation was a blazing success. They left New York's LaGuardia Field on a Colonial airliner at 9 a.m. Tuesday morning; arrived at Montreal's Dorval Airport at noon; met the mayor; were lunched and dined; exchanged cigarettes and military gossip with the CWACs; had more escorts (provided by the Canadian Fourth Military District) than they could dance with, at a party that night at the Mt. Royal Hotel.

But high point of the trip was the skiing. The girls had never been on skis before, were thrilled with glistening ski trails and crisp 18-inch snow which surrounded their Laurentian Mountains lodge. They took to Canadian winter like puppies, spent most of the time out of doors, practiced diligently, became so ski-facile that the usually reticent Canadians applauded madly.

CONTINUED ON NEXT PAGE 29

Chapter IX
The Home Front

It wasn't easy to read each day of the Nazis' progress in conquering Western Europe. Despair was deep indeed on June 10, 1940 when Mussolini brought Italy into the war, and deeper still in December 1941 when the Russians were valiant defending the eastern front.
—*USASOS WAKE UP, A TALE OF THE SOUTH PACIFIC*, Memoir by Vivian Paruta, WAC Technician 3rd Grade, Italian American

Vivian leaned toward Nicky and said, "This is our stop. It's only a couple of blocks from here." As they exited the bus, Nicky looked up and saw the massive clock tower and impressive dome. The building with its lavish embellishments appeared to be in the center of the city. "That's Paterson City Hall. It was modeled after the Hotel de Ville in France," Vivian told her.

There were rows of brick buildings with storefronts on the bottom floors. Children were playing stick ball in the streets. Women in head scarves carrying bags were going into the buildings. Small groups of boys were hanging out on the street corners.

"Welcome to Little Italy." Vivian pointed to a building across the street. "There it is."

An American flag was hanging in an ornate cast iron bracket. Below a sign read, *D. M. Paruta Imported and Domestic, Groceries 51 Market Street.* Billie Jean was taken over by all the sights, sounds and smells. There was strings of sausages, strands of garlic and fresh baked loaves of bread.

Inside, the grocery was filled with people speaking Italian. Some of the shelves were empty but others had boxes, cans and bottles with foreign labels she couldn't read. It was the day before Easter. In front of the meat counter stood a line of customers.

Billie Jean noticed a slightly overweight middle aged women with dark hair peppered with gray waving her arms. "Signor Paruta, I've been buying my meat here for over 10 years, you can make an exception for me."

"Signora Russo, why don't you ask your sister for her meat rations since you are preparing the Lamb for your family," he replied.

"Hi Papa," Vivian said with a quick nod, for she could see how busy he was. They walked back to the front of the store. Behind the cash register was a women who could have been Vivian in 25 years. "Nicky, I want to introduce you to my mama. Mama, this is Billie Jean. The girl I told you about."

Mrs. Paruta gave Nicky a warm smile and then began to check out the next customer in line. "Let's go on up to the apartment. I bet your hungry," said Vivian.

***

Instead of getting up before dawn to attend sunrise service, I attended mass the night before with Vivian. She called it the night of the Holy Saturday. St Michaels Roman Catholic Church was a beautiful house of worship, magnificent stain glass windows illuminated the sanctuary. I couldn't keep my eyes off the one of Mary and baby Jesus. Candles were lit everywhere. Organ music was playing.

The priests were dressed in long colorful robes with capes. One of the priests was swinging a large brass pot by a long chain. Smoke was pouring out as it moved from side to side filling the room. I had never seen such pageantry in a church service. Vivian called it High Holy Mass and said the entire liturgy would be in Latin. One of the Priest lit a candle and started chanting.

Vivian went up to the altar and was sprinkled with water. She told me when she came back that the candle symbolizes the Risen Christ and being sprinkled with holy water was a renewal of her baptism vows.

"What's holy water?" I asked.

"It's water blessed by the priest."

The whole thing ended with Holy Communion. I stayed seated since I wasn't Catholic and didn't know the rules. Walking back to the apartment, I felt like I had been bathed in some kind of ancient ritual.

Nothing like this exists back home and although I didn't understand any of the Latin, I sensed I had been touched in a strange and wonderful way.

***

Vivian's aunts and uncles arrived around noon. The women went directly to the kitchen while the men joined her father in the living room. I thought some things are the same no matter where you live. The table was beautifully set with white dishes on a yellow lace table cloth. Mr. Paruta apologized that he could not get the usual olives and cheeses from the old country but hoped that everyone enjoyed the salami and homemade mozzarella. He had put aside some anchovies for something called "antipasti."

I had no idea what an anchovy was and when I took a bite was surprised by the foul smell and overly salty taste. I could hardly swallow it but swallow I did. Vivian saw the face I made and starting laughing. Vivian's father brought out a Leg of Lamb which had been roasted with lemon and garlic. Bowls sitting on our plates were filled with asparagus soup. Red new potatoes with parsley steamed in the serving dish. What a spread of food! Vivian told me to try her aunt's mint jelly on one of the tiny biscuits. "It's the best," she said.

Mrs. Paruta insisted on beginning the meal with a prayer for Vivian's brothers who were serving overseas in Europe.

> Loving God you watch over each and every one of your children. Hear our prayer for Tony and Joe Be their constant companion Protect them no matter where they may go and bring them safely home to those who love them. Bless us Oh Lord, and these thy

gifts, which we are about to receive, from thy bounty, through Christ, Our Lord. Amen.

Everyone made the sign of the cross at the end of the blessing except for me. No one made any reference to Vivian and me serving in the Army. When Vivian mentioned that they were looking for WACs to serve under General MacArthur in the Pacific, a look of disbelief crossed her mother's face. Her aunt changed the subject, saying what a lovely meal they had provided given the rationing and scarcity of imported food. Vivian was visible upset. We took the train back to Fort Dix the next day.

Vivian and Nicky, Fort Dix NJ 1944

***

While at Fort Oglethorpe, Vivian had written Anthony her brother telling him she had joined the WACs, only to get a scolding letter back from him. He wrote that he could not believe with Joe away too, she would leave their mom and pop alone with the store. He said before he left to go overseas, he had seen some WACs in a tavern drunk and behaving badly and asked if she would want to be associated with those kinds of women.

Vivian took no time at all to set her brother straight and wrote him back a scathing letter stating he mustn't have thought much of her to think she would fall into that kind of thing. Tony must have known his sister was true blue but chose not to write back. They had a parting of the ways which would not mend for several years. Later he would regret having ever doubted her decision.

Vivian went home on every furlough while at Fort Dix. Even when Corky and Nicky pressed her to come to New York, she declined. After this last visit, she decided to apply for an overseas assignment. She was disillusioned with the Post Inspector General's office and said it was overstaffed with civilians. Corky and Nicky waved Vivian off as her train left the station to go back to Fort Oglethorpe for overseas training. A V-Mail arrived a month later from Camp Stoneman, California. Vivian would soon be leaving for Brisbane Australia on the SS *Lurine*.

On June 6th, D Day, Corky and Nicky put in their requests for overseas duty.

Chapter X
I Left My Heart in New York City

She saw him at the bottom of the stairs in the big hall at Grand Central. He gave her a smile slightly squinting his eyes causing his forehead to wrinkle. Jack had gotten them a room at the Paramount Hotel. It was too early to check in so they took a cab to Time Square.

Jean heard a familiar Gene Autry song but couldn't tell where it was coming from. "Look over there it's a Buster," said Jack. Jean didn't expect to hear cowboy music on the streets of New York. Around the Buster's neck hung a metal holder with a harmonica attached just like the one Woody Guthrie wore. He stopped singing but continued to strum his guitar, blowing, "You are My Sunshine." She started laughing. Her mama played that song. She could imagine her ma hanging cloths on the line while playing the tune on her mouth harp in that contraption.

The Diamond Horseshoe was in the basement of the Paramount. Jack had gotten tickets to the famous nightclub to surprise Jean. Billie Jean knew of Billy Rose and his famous Ziegfeld Girls. His outlandish shows were known from coast to coast. Helen and Fred told stories of going to the Casa Manana, Billy

Rose's club in Fort Worth. Fred raved about the clad clothed bare breasted cowgirl chorus line.

They descended the wide elaborate staircase to a Gay-Nineties themed saloon with deep red and white walls. Jack slipped the maître d' a five spot to make sure they got a table with a good view. He ordered Champaign.

Dressed in a long sequined gown standing in the middle of a spotlight, the vivacious soloist opened the floor show with a lively rendition of "Welcome to the Diamond Horseshoe." They were entertained by vaudeville reviews and tap dancing acrobats. The tall showgirls in feathered head dresses filled the stage for show stopping numbers. A chorus line of hefty over-sized women ended the cabaret in full Billy Rose burlesque style.

Jack couldn't keep his hands off her as they walked back to the room. Every time they turned a corner, he would pull her close and they would kiss. She could feel the weight of his body press against her. In the empty elevator he put his hand under her skirt. Jack moved his hand up her leg, he could feel the soft skin of her inner thigh, just above her stocking. He couldn't wait to get back to the room where he could unclip the fasteners and roll her silk stockings and panties down.

Finally reaching their room, he took out the key, unlocked the door and they went inside.

***

"Nicodemus, you have a phone call!" The shouting came from outside her barracks door. She walked down the hall to the pay phone mounted on the wall and picked up the hanging receiver. "Hello," she said having no idea who would be calling her so late.

"Jean, it's Jack," he said in a rushed almost panicked voice. Without a pause he continued, "I'm leaving tomorrow, goin' to California. I've been assigned to an Engineering Construction Battalion. We'll ship out to the Pacific next month." There was a long pause. "Jean, are you there?"

"Yes," she said. "I've requested overseas duty too. Major Hartleroad has written me a recommendation for Signal Intelligence."

Jean had the feeling she would never see or hear from Jack again. She had not told Jack that she was married, but had decided to tell him the next time they were together. It had been over a year since she had seen Nick. They still wrote to each other every month or so. She thought a divorce was eminent and had planned to ask him for one in her next letter. Everything was different now. The uncertainty of it all was overwhelming.

She cried herself to sleep.

***

It was a hot July afternoon when we arrived at the South Camp. Fort Oglethorpe was exactly the same as when I left. We were up at dawn for a two hour march. Marching and drills were the regiment for every day of our three week overseas training. Corky and I were partnered for the gas mask drill. With sweat running down our necks, we checked each other's masks to make sure they were a snug fit. The real test would be when we got our exposure to the tear gas.

Corky and Nicky during Gas Mask Training

The summer haze and smell of gas hung in the air. I could hardly make out my fellow WACS waiting in line. Looking through my goggles, everything was fuzzy and blurred. I felt light headed. We slowly walked up the steps leading to a building with boarded up windows. Our NCO was standing on the landing yelling instructions. "Walk into the center of the room, remove your mask and take a quick breath of the gas. Replace your mask as quickly as possible and try to breathe normally."

I gasped for air. My eyes burned and I became sick to my stomach but held it together. "Breathe normally," the Sergeant's instruction rang in my ears. I made my escape through a door on the opposite side. The WAC who came out of the gas chamber after me threw up in her mask. She had to repeat the drill. I was relieved that I only had to do it once.

We marched in the rain through the dense forest surrounding the post wearing heavy packs and steel helmets. We dug slit trenches for outdoor latrines. We practiced disembarking from landing crafts, climbing ropes like the ones used on the sides of ships. My long reach and long legs gave me an advantage over the shorter gals.

I was so busy and tired I rarely thought about Jack. But when I did, it hit me hard like running into that wall on the obstacle course.

The evening heat was stifling. We opened the windows and laid on our racks. I heard a beautiful echoing noise coming from across the big field. I realized that it must be coming from the German Prisoner of War Camp. I couldn't understand what they were singing but the soft deep harmony was pleasant and relaxing. For a moment I forgot about the heat and Jack. And that the voices coming from across the way were those of our enemy. The prisoners had been captured during the fall of North Africa, Afrika Korps soldiers serving under General Rommel.

When I saw the German prisoners working around the camp, I thought about Dub. Dub was out of the hospital and the Army had sent him back to the states for the duration. Helen wrote that he came home for R&R before being sent to Papago Park in Arizona. I thought it was odd that the Army would send him to the site of a large German Prisoner of War Camp after all he had been through. I worried about how Dub would do faced on a day to day basis with German POWs.

Helen said, Dub looked fine but was tight the whole time he was home. He spent all his money drinking and going to honky tonks. He was in a bar fight in Odessa and got all banged up. She said Jo Ann was really showing and would deliver in about a month. Come to find out, the daddy is married and has a little girl about a year old.

A few months back, Nick wrote in a letter he bumped in to Luke Gallagher at Ardmore. Luke had been promoted to 2nd Lieutenant and was now an instructor for a bomber squadron. He went back to Midland a couple of times to see Jo Ann. When she told him she was pregnant, he fessed up to being married. Jo Ann told everybody if the baby was a boy she didn't care what people thought she was going to name him, Luke Griffin after his daddy. I hope I can get back home before I go overseas.

PART THREE

O're the Foam She Roamed

Chapter XI
21 Days at Sea

A ship there is and she sails the sea
She's loaded deep as deep can be
But not so deep as the love I'm in
I know not if I sink or swim
— *The Water Is Wide, Scottish Folk Song*

Private Nicodemus approached the large wooden desk stopping with her feet together, eyes forward, frozen with a right hand salute, her best military form. The order to report to her Commander was concerning.

Lieutenant Colonel Strayhorn glanced up to meet the WAC's salute and then returned to her reading. She looked up at the tall young woman standing at attention, then down at the paper and then back at her before saying, "At ease Private. Major Hartleroad gave you a glowing recommendation." Nicky thought of her last meeting with the Major and the strange question he asked. "Do you like crossword puzzles?" "Yes sir, I find them fun and challenging," she answered.

She worked six months under the Major, a stand out in the stenography pool at Fort Dix. Her dictation and typing were near perfect. She easily picked up the skills needed for every new piece of office equipment thrown at her including the teletype. When Lieutenant Helen Baker, the WAC Special Service officer mentioned that the Private had requested an overseas assignment, Hartleroad thought that she would fit the bill. Quiet and highly focused, she had top notch scores and was of outstanding character.

Major Hartleroad was given the task to recommend capable WAC for the highly secretive Signal Intelligence Service. The war was ramping up in the Pacific and the SIS was desperate for men and women. The WAAC of the Signal Security Agency had proven themselves most capable and the need for personnel was critical.

Nicky looked down at her orders. She would not get to go home before leaving to go overseas. Her next appointment was Special Troops General Headquarters, Asiatic Pacific. She was told she had been selected for a special assignment but nothing more. Lieutenant Colonel Strayhorn was explicit she was to tell no one anything about her orders, not even her family. She would be court marshaled if she did. Only after she arrived at her new post could she ask permission to send them her APO address.

***

Corky and I boarded the L & N train in Chattanooga not knowing where we were going. We suspected that we would be deployed from California but no information was given to us. We were told we would operate on a need to know basis. The alphabetical system used to assign berths put Corky and me in different sleeping cars. We got together as much as we could sitting in the club car watching the world go by while drinking coffee and having a smoke.

We boarded a troop train in St. Louis heading west to Denver traveling though the beautiful Rocky Mountains. The barren land of Utah and Nevada reminded me of home, not a respectable tree in sight and you could see forever. The beautiful sunset on the salt flats was hypnotizing. When we reached California, a few of us heard *The Presidio* would be our destination. Camp Stoneman, the army staging area typically used for deployment to the Pacific was filled to the gills.

I was relieved that Corky and I would remain together. We were housed in temporary quarters until our deployment. Waking up at sunrise was amazing. Outside our quarters you could see a blanket of fog hanging low over the San Francisco Bay, hovering below the Golden Gate Bridge. I watched as the fog moved over the city as if a mother was gently pulling a cover over her baby. It was August but surprisingly cool. Our wool uniforms were much appreciated.

In a few days I would be leaving this magnificent bay. I felt free and proud. I had crossed this expansive country, New Jersey to Georgia and Georgia to San Francisco. Now I would cross the Pacific. Foghorns woke me the morning of our departure. The random melody seemed to be calling me out to sea. Droplets ran down the window as I looked out to the bay. I had lived almost my entire life in the desert and now I would be surrounded by water for weeks with possibly no land in sight.

We got our gear and headed for the mess hall for a hardy breakfast of SOS, 'Shit on a Shingle.' The infamous Army grub consisted of biscuits with sausage gravy. The greasy chow did not settle well in my stomach but I had no idea how I would yearn for the mild rumblings in the coming week.

I stood on the dock looking up at the gigantic ship. She appeared to be about the length of two football fields. The SS Lurline was a beauty, our transport to the Asiatic Pacific and adventure beyond. The ocean liner had been converted to a troopship for the duration of the war. A thousand others joined us, GIs and WACs arrived from Camp Stoneman. We waited for hours before boarding. Soon, we would find out that the luxurious ocean liner would be striped of most of her lavishness to make way for service men and women and the repeated journeys crossing the Japanese infested waters.

Corky and I exited the gang plank on to the ship and were directed way down in the hold to our staterooms. Corky and I were put in different rooms. My cabin was extremely small and had been outfitted with eight bunks crammed together in two rows that went all the way up to the ceiling. There were 4 gals standing around and chatting in that tiny space. I noticed another sitting on one of the bottom bunks working a crossword puzzle. I would soon find out that all six of us had been given the same special orders.

The girl working the crossword puzzle glanced up and said, "Hi, they call me, Alabama." I recognized the familiar southern lilt. "They call me, Nicky," I said returning her engaging smile.

Before we could speak any further, we were interrupted by the public address system, "Now hear this, all WACs on D deck report immediately with your mess kits to the dining area on E deck."

Pfc. Ruth B. Newsome, AKA "Alabama"

Enlisted personnel were standing in the halls pointing us in the direction for our first meal on ship. Alabama and I caught up with Corky in the large dining room. After getting our kits filled with boiled potato and canned peaches, we parked ourselves at the end of one of the long tables. Alabama told us that she was recruited for the Signal Corps while in College and joined after completing her degree in English. She had gotten her special training in New Jersey at Fort Monmouth.

We spent most of our time on the Promenade deck to fend off the stifling heat. To fight off the nausea, we put our heads between our knees. The back and forth and up and down motion was never ending. We zig zagged all over that ocean to avoid Japanese submarines. I asked one of the sailors how they knew where the Jap subs were and he said there was a big machine below decks that did that.

Alabama told me later in private they used something called a magnetometer that measured variations in the magnetic field and could detect large metal objects like submarines.

We were jammed in the dining room, ready to watch a movie to pass the time. Everyone looked up when we heard the familiar rapid clicking of the film moving through the projector sprockets. **United News** flashed on the screen with an update on General MacArthur's progress in the Southwest Pacific.

"Striking suddenly in the Southwest Pacific, General MacArthur leads combined sea, air, and land forces against the Admiralty Islands, just north of New Guinea," declared the male broadcaster. Other than hear say the only way we got our news regarding the war or what was happening on the home front was from these short newsreels on movie night. The newscaster continued, "A shattering naval bombard-ment covers the landing as the General observes the action from the flagship. Meeting little initial resistance, U.S. cavalrymen, trained to fight as infantry, storm the beach. Their objective: Momote Airfield, new base from which to strike new blows at the enemy, now being encircled on nearby Rabaul.

Landing eight hours after the invasion, General MacArthur inspects American positions and congratulates his troops. To the north, on Eniwetok in the Marshall Islands, mechanized forces win another vital Jap outpost. Islanders huddle for safety under the protection of American guns as the occupation of the island is completed. This is the pattern of war in the Pacific. Another victory that puts the Allied forces one step nearer to Tokyo."

General MacArthur was obsessed with recapturing the Philippines. The importance of dominating and securing key islands in the Pacific was pivotal in accomplishing this goal. Early strategic victories like the Battle of the Coral Sea and the Battle of Midway were well documented in the military war films and newsreels. The recent triumphs of securing the Marshal Islands and the hard fought battles at Papua and Dutch New Guinea were fresh on everyone's minds. The troops crossing the ocean knew they would be serving under General Douglas Mac Arthur, Supreme Commander of the Southwest Pacific Area and they would do their part, whatever it took.

***

I stood on the promenade deck as we approached Papua, New Guinea. A white sandy beach laid beyond the dark blue water. Gray jagged mountain peaks were in the distance. It reminded me of a forbidden land in a Grimm fairy tale. It was hauntingly beautiful.

Most of the troops including Corky, disembarked at Oro Bay, Papua New Guinea. I remained on the ship because I was under special orders to go to Brisbane, Australia. I felt sad not knowing when I might see her again. We had become inseparable ever since Corky had named me "Nicky" back at Fort Oglethorpe.

As we pulled further and further away from shore I felt a separateness magnified by the near emptiness of the ship. Besides my cabin mates, only the crew and a few officers were left on board. I had no idea why we were the only ones moving on to Brisbane.

Chapter XII
A Heightened Sense of Security
September 1944

THE SUITCASE
BACK HOME WHERE I CAME FROM
A SUITCASE MEANT A TRIP
A VACATION, AN OUTING
WHERE YOU DIDN'T GIVE A RIP

BUT IN THE LAND DOWN UNDER
IT'S NOT LIKE THAT AT ALL
FOR HERE THEY ALL CARRY THEM
THE BIG GUY AND THE SMALL

MY CURIOSITY RUNS RAMPAGE
WHEN I SEE THEM ON THE STREET
MORNING, NOON AND NIGHT THEY COME
WITH THAT SUITCASE BY THEIR FEET

THE SCHOOL BOY BACK HOME
WHO TIES HIS BOOKS WITH STRAPS
WOULD HERE BE OUT OF FASHION
TO CARRY THEM ON HIS LAP

THE BUSINESS MAN AT HOME
WHO TAKES TIME OUT FOR HIS CHOW
AND RUSHES TO A SWANKY PLACE
TO EAT WITH MUCH FAN-FARE
WOULD FIND IT VERY HARD TO EAT

WITH A SUITCASE UPON HIS KNEE
WHERE AS YOU KNOW
OUR BUSINESS MAN
EXPECTS A SECRETARY TO BE

WHEN THE WOMEN GO A SHOPPING
THERE TOO THE SUITCASE MUST GO
WHERE FOR HATS OR BEANS OR BERRIES
OR JUST TO CATCH A BEAU

SO HERE'S TO THE LAND DOWN UNDER
TO EVERY SUITCASE IN THE LAND
LONG MAY THEY CARRY THEIR BURDEN
FOR THIS AUSTRALIAN CLAN

AND WHEN THE WAR IS OVER
AT THE PEACE TABLE I'LL EXPECT TO SEE
A MAN FROM DOWN UNDER
WITH A SUITCASE BY HIS KNEE

—*"ALABAMA"*

It was a pleasant sunny afternoon when Alabama and I boarded the double decker bus and left the Port of Brisbane. I've always wanted to ride in a double decker ever since I saw a picture of one in *Life Magazine*. This one was painted a drab camouflage not the cheery red and white I dreamed of riding someday in London.

"Look at that, Nicky. They're all carrying suitcases," said Alabama as she leaned out the upper deck window. There was a woman with a suitcase in one hand and a small child in the other standing outside a grocery. On the street corner, a group of school boys all dressed alike in their dark jackets and khaki shorts carried brown leather strapped cases. Trotting along the sidewalk was a man in a business suit and hat with an oversized bag in hand, rushing like he was trying to catch a ride but with no train or bus stop in sight. I wondered why in the world they were toting around heavy suitcases.

We drove through the brick gates of Yeronga Park and down Honor Avenue. The road was lined with tall trees planted for those who had died in the Great War. A metal plate was placed on each tree carrying an individual name of the military dead. Long tree shadows were cast by the late afternoon sun. You could have heard a pin drop as we pasted through the memorial and turned on to Ipswick Road.

Some of the trees had pitted marks with missing bark. It gravely saddened me to learn our boys were using the trees for bayonet practice. Timber fences reinforced with barbwire surrounded the large encampment. It had all the Army essentials, a formal parade ground with flagpole, Post Exchange, Infirmary, Recreation Hut and open-air Cinema.

After getting something to eat at the mess hall, we were assigned to our living quarters. We walked along white painted stone paths to our barracks. These paths were used to get around the Post reducing the need for flashlights and would prove especially helpful during air-raid blackouts. Our barracks were huts with metal corrugated roofs and long wooden windows which opened outward. We would sleep on cots. Our digs were comfortable enough I thought, until I was shown the bucket latrines and outdoor showers.

The next day we were taken to Victoria Park. We drove under a sign that read Base Section USASOS. U.S. Army Service of Supplies was where Vivian was assigned. All the enlisted WACs were quartered at Yeronga Park, so it would only be a matter of time before I bumped in to her.

I was not told where I would be stationed, only that I had special orders to USAFFE, U.S. Army Forces in the Far East. Victoria Park was bustling with rows of long one story buildings with metal roofs and military vehicles everywhere. Two by fours held several buildings off the ground to allow for runoff and flash floods during the rainy season. Today, it looked bone dry. We would soon learn that every piece of U.S. Army supplies requisitioned for the Pacific from nail files to tanks came through the USASOS, most right here at Victoria Park.

***

We were on Post no time at all when our group of six was ordered on to another truck. We headed out of the military complex driving through a residential district. We turned into a flat, grassy area. I noticed a small sign that read Ascot Park.

A tall attractive officer in her early thirties was waiting outside what appeared to be a Fire Station. It didn't look like a military facility at all. The red brick building with gabled roof was modest in size and was set among some lovely trees. The officer was smartly dressed in her pinks and greens wearing a garrison cap with her dark brown hair neatly pinned back.

Captain Margaret Turner walked up to us and returned our salute. We made our introductions. She took us inside and said, "Newsome and Nicodemus, you wait here." The others followed the Captain down the hall exiting right. We heard a low frequency rhythmic thumping noise as we waited.

Cpt. Margaret Turner

She returned and took us to the back of the building through a room filled with machines. The rhythmic thumping got louder. I had never seen such a site. The equipment appeared to be some kind of sorting apparatuses, each having thirteen slots that organized these large manila cards. The cards had multiple small holes in them. The Captain took us to a very small room with no windows. There was a desk and a couple of chairs with a wall poster of a WAAC with her pointed finger placed on her mouth indicating the hush sign, SILENCE MEANS SECURITY written on the bottom. Captain Turner told us to sit down as she leaned against the desk.

"You have been assigned to Central Bureau Brisbane, Signal Intelligence, code word SIGINT." She spelled out SIGINT. "What you learn, know, see and hear should never be spoken of outside your unit. Everything that happens here is top secret. If you are caught discussing anything outside your SIGINT station, it will be considered an act of treason during a time of war and you will be punished to the full extent of the law." Alabama and I knew that could mean prison or even execution.

Captain Turner took a deep breath and continued. "Before we get into details you need to understand the vital importance of what we do and how essential it is to winning this war. You have been chosen for this work because of your abilities and discretion. Captain Turner shook her head and looked at us as if thinking we just might do.

***

Back at Arlington Hall, Margaret never dreamed she would be delegated to assemble her own cryptologic field unit. She needed to fill the last two spots. There were two WACs in the latest arrivals that appeared to have what she was looking for.

When Margaret Turner was offered an assignment to work with the eminent SIS mathematician, Lieutenant Colonel Abraham Sinkov, Commander of the Central Bureau in Brisbane, she accepted right away. It was the opportunity she had hoped for, to go to the Pacific. Deliah Sinkov, one of her instructors at

Arlington Hall, would talk proudly of her husband's position and contribution to the effort.

In 1930, Abraham Sinkov and his high school friend Solomon Kullback were hand selected by William F. Friedman, the brilliant pioneer in cryptology, to join the newly formed Army's Signal Intelligence Service. Both had studied mathematics and foreign language at New York's famed City College. The small group of Junior Cryptanalysts initially consisted of only four which included another mathematician with voluble German, Frank Rowlett, and John Hurt a young man unusually fluent in Japanese. Later the team expanded adding a select group of women, Wilma Zimmerman, Genevieve Grotjan, Mary Jo Dunning and Abraham's wife, Deliah.

Margaret Turner's background in mathematics and language served her well in her training back in Virginia. She quickly moved through the communications intelligence, COMIT courses in translation, interception traffic analysis and cryptology. Margaret was known as Peggy to all her classmates. Peggy worked tirelessly sometimes 16 hours a day decoding enciphered messages. Her experience breaking high-level encrypted enemy radio and teleprint communications known as ULTRA would prove to be invaluable in her new assignment.

While at Arlington Hall, there were several woman cryptanalysts she admired. Significant breakthroughs enabling the SIS to solve critical diplomatic Japanese codes were accomplished by women. The Cryptologist she admired most was Genevieve Grotjan whose hard work and discoveries made it possible to build an analog machine that solved the Japanese diplomatic code system known as "Purple." Breaking the Purple code provided crucial intelligence in the Pacific and Atlantic theaters.

Peggy's razor-sharp intelligence, work ethic and pleasant nature quickly endeared her to many of her instructors. It was a close knit group. Once at a SIS officers' cocktail party, she was privileged to meet Frank Rowlett, the most senior cryptanalyst except for Friedman himself. When Genevieve Grotjan walked in the room, he went right in to a story about how they broke the Purple code.

"Finally, Genevieve found the evidence we were looking for. It was around 2 p.m. Ferner, Small and I were working discussing prospects and reviewing work. Grotjan entered the room, obviously excited in her mild manner way. She politely interrupted, asking if she could show us what she had found. She took us to her desk in the next room, laid out her worksheets, pointed to one example, then another, then a third. She stood back, with eyes tranced behind her rimless glasses.

Al Small dashed around the room, hands clasped above his head like a victorious prizefighter. 'Whoopee!' he yelled. Ferner, you know how quiet he is, clasped his hands, shouting 'Hooray, Hooray.' I jumped up and down. 'That's it! That's it!' Friedman came in and asked, 'What's all the noise about?'"

He knew the story would embarrass Gene but when he looked across the room at her flushed face, he raised his glass to her and said, "Good Show."

***

Two WACs walked into the undersized office, both Technician 5th Grade rank. They looked like they could have been sisters, same height, same weight, same cropped hair and eye color. Their expressions were even the same. "Kathy and Lora will show you the ropes and train you on the punchers," said the Captain.

Kathy and Lora had been in the Army since the Women's Auxiliary days. They met at Vint Hill Farms in Virginia where they got their intelligence training. "We receive the intercepted encrypted messages by teletype." Lora shouted over the mechanical clamoring as she pointed to the bank of teletype machines against the wall.

The deafening noise was coming from the puncher machines which were arranged in rows of two, five deep. WACs and GIs were seated behind the machines busily typing. A manila card was in a track held up on a metal stand about eye level. Each time a key was hit a hole was punched in the card by a moving carriage sitting above. When the card was completed it slid to the right and was manually placed in a card holder. A new card was manually put in the track from a stack to the left.

Lora walked us to what she called, "the IBM room." It was the room we had walked through on our arrival. "After a message is punched on the cards, they are taken here to be sorted, collated and printed. The sorter and tabulator machines produce a variety of sorts, alphabetical and numerical. After the sorting, it is the tabulators that add, subtract and summarize the totals and then prints out the tabulated reports. The Cryptanalysts are looking for patterns in the code to match with previous codes or the daily code. The cards help to identify these patterns more quickly."

She held up a stack of cards to the light and you could see that some of the holes were perfectly aligned by the light shining through. The rooms hummed with efficiency and Jean was impressed by the precision of it all. Captain Turner walked up to Lora. Jean noticed that no saluting or military formalities were exchanged. "Lora, I need your help. Kathy can get them started on the punchers."

Kathy began her explanation. "For experienced typists like yourselves you'll find this easy. Remember accuracy is of the utmost importance and speed the next. Error cards are repunched. The punchers are made by Remington Rand. They also make the 45 caliber military sidearm."

Nicky and Alabama each sat behind a puncher. Nicky looked at the teletype page. There were rows of what looked like random digits grouped in fours. Standing in front of the machines, Kathy began her instruction. "The keyboard is almost exactly like one on a typewriter, except the shift, tab and backspace keys are eliminated. Oh yah, the character key is eliminated too like on the Mil typewriter.

"There are 80 columns numbered left to right on a IBM card and 12 rows from top to bottom," Kathy said as she ran her finger across the card. "Numbers are punched as 0 through 9 but alphabetic characters are punched in a code sequence, A is a 12 punch and a 1 punch, B is a 12 punch and a 2 punch, C a 12 and 3 and so forth." She indicated all the alphabetical sequences on the card.

Kathy was right, punching came easily. In the weeks to come, we would perfect our keypunching skills and complete training on how to run the sorters and tabulators. There was a mix of men and women. I noticed immediately the working conditions were informal not like at Fort Dix where rank and military protocol were strictly observed. Officers and enlisted worked side by side in every aspect of the operation. Everyone was on a first name basis. Captain Turner told us to call her "Peggy." She seemed amused when we told her to call us "Nicky" and "Alabama."

At the end of the day, I had an opportunity to chat with an Australian corporal over coffee while we waited for a ride back to Yeronga Park. He was a friendly guy, maybe he was flirting. Anyhow, I asked him, "What was it with all the civilians carrying suitcases?"

"You ever heard of the Brisbane Line," he asked? I shook my head. "Banana-benders believe," he paused when he saw the question look on my face. "Folks round here believe when the Japanese cross the Brisbane Line just to the north the government will abandon Queensland. Ever since the Japs moved into New Guinea, Queenlanders think it's a matter of time. Right that'd be with their ports, ready to leave."

Chapter XIII
Aussieland

AUSSIE LAND
This is the land down under
Where things work in reverse,
And you're apt to make a blunder,
In ways that I'll rehearse.

Where Winter comes in Summer
And Spring appears in Fall,
Don't ever ask for "spirits"
The military's got it all.

Where a "cobber" is a "buddy"
And a streetcar is a "tram"
Where the favorite word is "bloody"
And it's equal to our "damn".

Where a druggist is a "chemist"
And a tavern is a "pub"
Where a "smoogie" is a kiss
And the women call you "love".

Where they always say "fair dinkum"
When they mean a thing's "O.K."
Where they say "t'will be a fortnight"
When they mean two weeks away.

In the language of the Aussies,
A Yank's a "bonzer bloke"
If he reaches in his pocket
And says "Digger" have a smoke.

A "Digger" is a soldier
And he drinks his beer from kegs;
I guess I haven't told you,
That they all eat "stike and eggs."

Where a stranger must be careful
For his life's in dangerous plight
And to add to his confusion
What should be left is right.

Where a pleasant surprise awaits you
Though astonishing it might be
They'll give you a seven-course dinner
When they ask you in for tea.

Roughly, that's the land down under,
Please don't misunderstand;
But you're apt to make a blunder
When you come to Aussieland.
—*Unknown WAC*

It had been a long 16-hour double shift, my neck was stiff and eyes tired. Peggy handed me a 24-hour pass as I left to go back to my quarters to get some mid-morning shut eye. Which meant 40 hours before I had to report back. When I got to my hut I could hardly stand. I collapsed on my bed fully clothed and fell asleep. "Nicky, wake up! We're going to the SIS Club," yelled Sally, a new puncher at the Bureau.

I jumped from my cot, threw on a fresh khaki shirt and skirt. Ran a brush through my hair and put on some red lipstick. We hopped on the tram at the end of Ipswick Road just outside the camp and headed for the club.

As we approached the door, we could hear the lively drinking song, the robust chorus kept getting louder and louder. The entire house erupted to sing the refrain.

"Waltzing Matilda, Waltzing Matilda"
"You'll come a-Waltzing Matilda, with me"

Aussie voices joined in unison for the verse.

"And he sang as he watched and waited till his billy boiled
You'll come a-Waltzing Matilda, with me
Down came a jumbuck to drink at that billabong,
Up jumped the wagman and grabbed him with glee
And he sang as he shoved that jumbuck in his tucker bag,
You'll come a Waltzing Matilda, with me"

Aussies and Americans were singing at the top of their lungs, some arm n' arm. We waited until the joyful noise was over before we made our way in.

There was a band of Aussies standing by a keg at the back of the room. "Look over there, its Woodie. She sure looks rugged, too much Aussie beer, huh, or maybe just tired. You know Woodie, she usually works the graveyard shift," I said to Sally. SIGINT WAAAFs, Women's Australian Auxiliary Air Force also worked at the Bureau.

Australian SigInts at the SIS Club, Brisbane 1944

Woodie was an unusual looking gal, short and stocky, round flattish face with hair of thick tight curls. She was surrounded by, SISers from the Royal Australian Air Force and other WAAAFs in skirted fatigues and flowers in their hair. She motioned us over.

One of the guys tapped us a beer. "Fair dinkum," he said as he handed us our glasses. We could hear from across the room one of the RAAFs giving a toast, "Here's to the bloody yanks, they'll save our arses." Who would have ever guessed that these SIGINTs could be such a rowdy bunch?

***

It took a few weeks to finally arrange leave with Vivian. We decided to make a day of it sightseeing. Vivian told me Brisbane reminded her of Paterson. "The city hall has a clock tower like back home and European style architecture is everywhere." We took the tram traveling along the South Bank crossing the river by the Victoria Bridge. We got off on Edward Street and started walking down Ann Street.

The Greek style monument with its sandstone columns encircled a brass urn containing an Eternal Flame. *The Shrine of Remembrance* sat on top of a crypt which held the memories of those fallen in war. With the memorial behind us, we stood on the granite steps looking down on the square. The grounds were perfectly manicured. ANZA Square was a place of homage to the Australian and New Zealand Army Corps. We made our way down a wide footpath lined with palm trees heading toward a bronze statue of an Australian soldier on horseback.

We headed to the Brisbane City Hall at King George Square. Vivian wanted to show me the clock tower and the stunning auditorium with the circular hall covered by a large copper dome. We turned back toward Edwards Street and looked up at a nine story building on the corner of Queens Street.

"That's MacArthur Central, the Southwest Pacific Headquarters," she whispered.

I had met a couple of stenographers back at Yeronga who said they worked at MacArthur Central. That's the hub where General Douglas MacArthur and his senior staff were making crucial decisions for the campaign to take back the Philippines.

I had yet to experience the impact of being a soldier but I couldn't help but feel the effects of war all around me. Memorials to soldiers lost, overhead stories by those who had served in battle and of course the suitcase companions carried by locals. GIs were all over the place playing tourist like Vivian and I, grabbing moments of Australian hospitality.

The buildings on Queens Street were lovely, massive stone structures with arched windows. We gawked at the large columns and wide ornate balconies that over looked the street. One of the buildings housed several retail stores which included a grocery store named *Manahans* and a drug store named *Chemist Roush*. Before we entered

Manahans, Vivian pointed to a marquee across the street that read.

NOW SHOWING PRIDE AND PREJUDICE
LAURENCE OLIVIER
GREER GARSON

"Let's go, that's a magnificent theatre," she said. We grabbed two bottles of coke and placed them on the counter. "G'day, Love, can I help you?" said the woman behind the register. I gave her money for the cokes and asked, "I noticed the sign *Regent Studio*. Is that a portrait studio?" "Yes, Love, it's on the second floor." I wanted to get a professional portrait taken in my uniform before I left the States but the Army had me out and on my way before I could do it. Maybe I could get one made here on my next leave.

A line was already forming outside *The Regent*. The theatre had the same name as the photography studio above the grocery. There was lively chatter by GIs and Australians waiting to buy tickets. I could hardly understand the chitchat because of the heavy Aussie accents. There was "digger" this and "digger" that. One Australian soldier asked his date for a "smoogie" at which she immediately planted a big one right on his lips.

A stocky round faced Australian GI walked up to us with his mate in tow. "You ladies want to blow the froth off a few coldies at the pub down the street after the film," he asked? We told him we had to head back to the base and thanked him for the invite.

It was an American style picture palace much like the ones in big cities back home. It was larger and classier than the Yucca. The auditorium had a high vaulted ceiling with French ornamental plaster walls. A Wurlitzer organ sat beside a stage draped in heavy velvet curtains with gold bouquet.

We thoroughly enjoyed the lighthearted movie. It stayed true to the foyer poster's claim as *The Gay Comedy Hit*. Vivian had read the book and said the movie had played lavishly with the plot and time period but she thought it was fun and very entertaining. I identified with the story of the five sisters and loved the elaborate over the top costumes. The long kiss between Elizabeth played by Greer Garson and Mr. Darcy played by Laurence Olivier was a perfect ending.

We decided to head back to camp after the movie. It had been a full day and we were wore out. I needed a good night's sleep before I reported early in the morning for another double shift.

Chapter XIV
Dutch, New Guinea
October 1944

New Guinea
> There things I love – the quietness
> of coming eventide –
> When shadows start to lengthen
> and the moon begins its ride.
> The darkness over comes us;
> it is the close of day.
> The sun retreats behind the rim
> in a mysterious way.
> The land is cloaked in darkness,
> with ethereal shrouded bliss,
> A sweet nocturnal air prevails
> from out the vast abyss.
> The stars are here-each one is clear.
> The studded sky is jeweled
> With points of light that make it bright.
> With this, the world's imbued.
> The stalwart mountains guarding,
> their lonely vigil keep,
> Watching all humanity
> while it is deep in sleep.
> Put look, arise, the sun appears
> from out the great beyond.

> And lo, the very night has fled
> and darkness turns to dawn.
> The day in its entire splendor
> comes forth in bright array.
> The stars are gone – the darkness, too.
> It is another day.
> —*Unknown WAC, New Guinea 1944-1945*

Three weeks after we had arrived at the Central Bureau, Captain Turner called Alabama and me into her office. "I have selected you to be in my field unit with Kathy and Lora. We will be sent to Hollandia, New Guinea to serve in the Rear Echelon."

Sitting on her desk was an 8 by 6 inch book with a reddish brown cover. Peggy picked up the book and opened it so we could see the text. Our Captain said that she needed to train us in all aspects of decoding used in the field. "In Hollandia we will be given specific deciphering or processing assignments. We may need to decrypt intercepts ourselves on the spot, depends on the urgency and complexity. Deciphered messages can be sent on for translations or if translations are fairly straight forward, we will do it ourselves using Japanese code books like this one, passing on what we find directly to our immediate command."

Each page of the code book had three columns of 4 digit sequential numbers. A space beside each number contained Japanese characters with the occasional alphabet letter or number. A few numbers had nothing beside them while some had handwritten English word translations added. "We will receive monthly or bimonthly rebuilt code books to stay as current as possible to the changing code," she said.

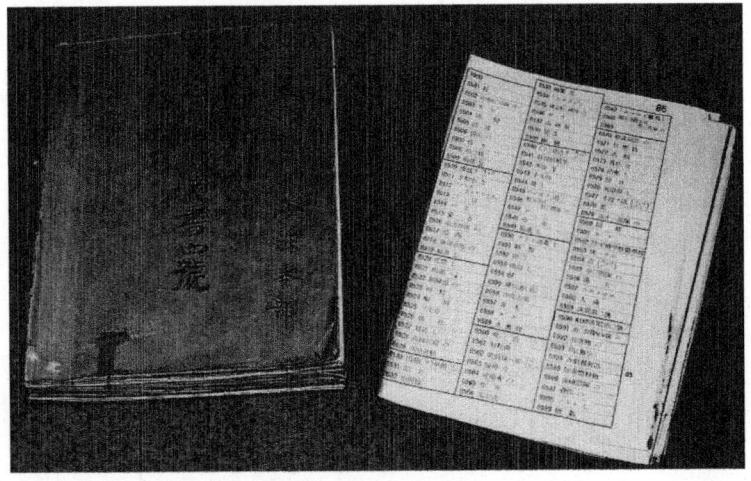

Japanese Code Book, photo courtesy of the National Cryptologic Museum

The Japanese naval codes were unlike German codes. They were primarily "book" ciphers, while German codes used mechanical encipherment, as in the famous Enigma and Lorenz machines. With book ciphers, the sender composes his message and then consults the code book. Common words and phrases were replaced with groups of numbers and letters, and any remaining text encoded character by character. The resulting coded message was then transmitted. The receiver then looks up each group in the corresponding code book and reassembles the message.

The main Japanese naval code, The Navy General Operational Code, dubbed JN25 by the U.S., had a code book of 90,000 words and phrases. Even after individual phrases and words were decoded the meaning and significance of them had to be inferred in order to understand the entire message. For this reason, breaking the code was an art requiring technical skill, imagination, and a knack for solving puzzles.

"Breaking" Japanese coded messages was essentially an exercise in puzzle-solving. The meaning of a particular code group could be inferred by context or by cross-referencing its use in other messages. Code breakers were known for their prodigious memories, using specific code groups. The end result was a huge card catalog representing the inferences and deductions of code groups of the JN25 code book. A common practice in "breaking" codes was to look for "cribs," or phrases routinely used in Japanese messages such as "I have the honor to inform your Excellency." The Japanese carelessly used the same phrases routinely in their coded transmissions, allowing the cryptologists to determine the code for these phrases and use it to decipher the remainder of the message.

Peggy gave us keywords to help us decipher the multiple four-figures pointing out clues that might help within the messages themselves. "Notice that most of these messages follow a set pattern giving the name of the ship, location, commander, time and date, right at the beginning. Nice of the Japanese to do that," she said.

We quickly learned to identify repetitive phrases or words used in the messages. Sometimes we could determine the meaning ourselves with the given keywords and codebook information. But more often we would identify the repeated patterns and send them on to be analyzed or interpreted. She told us the Japanese had been careless in many ways when they departed after the Battle of Midway. Burned code books were found partially intact which provided cipher information on the JN40 Japanese Merchant Shipping Code giving invaluable entry into their code system. "It is essential for you to remember how important it is to completely destroy all scrap paper and worksheets at the end of your shift. All code books and notebooks will be locked up and secured. SIGINT has burning stations out back for waste papers."

***

Vivian got orders to move to Hollandia. She was placed in the Advance Echelon as a stenographer. I met Vivian at her barracks to say good bye the night before she left. Her Royal typewriter was sitting on her cot. "I was told to take it with me and that it would accompany me wherever I'm stationed from now on. I'll think of it as my gun," she lightheartedly said.

It would be less than a week when Vivian and I saw each other again. My unit flew out on a C-47 for Dutch, New Guinea. The plane was loaded with supplies and us as human cargo. We dropped altitude while crossing the Netherland East Indies in to a valley of lush green mountains. A little village of thatched huts lay below. I could barely make out the small dark native people staring up at us. We landed on a huge inland airstrip at the foot of a mountain. A couple of Jeeps were waiting to take us to Hollandia. We threw our duffle bags in and held on for dear life as we rode the bumpy thirty miles.

We reached the coastline covered in dirt. I shook the dust from my hair, wiped the filth from my eyes and mouth and peered out upon a strip of golden sand. In the background were blue mountains rising out of the sea. Coconut palms were gently leaning toward the shoreline, a South Seas paradise. We pulled over.

"That's Imbi beach," our driver said. "See the GIs out there swimming in the surf, our headquarters for R&R. Now that we have some women around, I bet ya we'll have more beer parties and barbeques."

The whole time Jean had been in the army, she was never asked if she could swim. She was deathly afraid of the water, little opportunity to learn in West Texas. The SS Lurine was so big she didn't think much about it except during the life boat drills. She would enjoy a party on the beach just as long as no one asked her to go for a swim.

The jungle butted right up to the beach. Huge lacy ferns sprung up from the ground. Tangled vines hung everywhere, latching on to trees, reaching out from branches as if looking for strangers to take hold of. Enormous trees with leathery leaves dominated the jungle. Their massive twisted roots protruded out of black oozy mud. From the huge branches, long sister roots hung to the ground. One was coiled like a snake around a small Palm tree. Our driver called the ancient trees "Banyans." "One of the oldest trees on Earth. They're known as strangling figs," he said.

After our beach drive, we entered the base along the harbor. There were ships and boats of all sizes. Navy and Army installations lined the dock. Finally, we reached Base G. Tall chicken-wire fencing surrounded the stark WAC compound. Two imposing MPs guarded the entrance. We drove past the mess hall, orderly room and a newly constructed recreation building. I saw a group of tents and a lake in the distance with cloud topped mountains.

"What's that?" I asked our driver nodding towards the tents. "Your quarters," he replied. "That's Sentani Lake and the Cyclops Mountains in the distance." I could tell this would be a land of contrasts, wartime necessities thrown against magnificent beauty. I made out three women of varying heights standing by the first tent. I squinted to make out the short WAC standing in the middle. To my surprise, it was my petite Italian pal waving at me.

Vivian told us of her exciting arrival. "On landing, we caught the eye of a soldier who said we were the first women he'd seen in several months. He offered us a ride in his jeep, and we eagerly accepted. He headed for the beach, a restricted zone, where there were units in formation ready to embark for action on near-by islands." As she continued, I thought stepping stones to the Philippines. "It was a sight, soldiers in full fighting gear standing at ease with their beer rations at their feet, landing craft nearby with the unknown rolling sea beyond."

She led us to our barracks. The jungle had been hacked away from the surrounding premises. "The showers and latrines are over there," Vivian pointed to the outdoor facilities.

Our quarters were the most primitive I'd seen. A trench was dug around the outside of our tent. I noticed a beat up helmet sat in the corner of the room half full of water. There were four canvas cots set up in a fifteen foot square area. "Nicky, it's not so bad it just takes a little getting used to," Vivian said when she saw the look on my face. "The 239th will build us a proper bath house soon." I dragged my duffel across the dirt floor to one of the cots.

***

After breakfast, we walked down to the recreational building to take a look around. There were two GIs inside the newly erected hall. "We're with the 239th Engineering Construction Battalion and we'd like you to come to our dance on Saturday night," a skinny red haired PFC said handing us a paper. His enthusiasm made us laugh. The typed invitation was on a half sheet of paper folded so the text was on the left inside page instead of the typical right. It read:

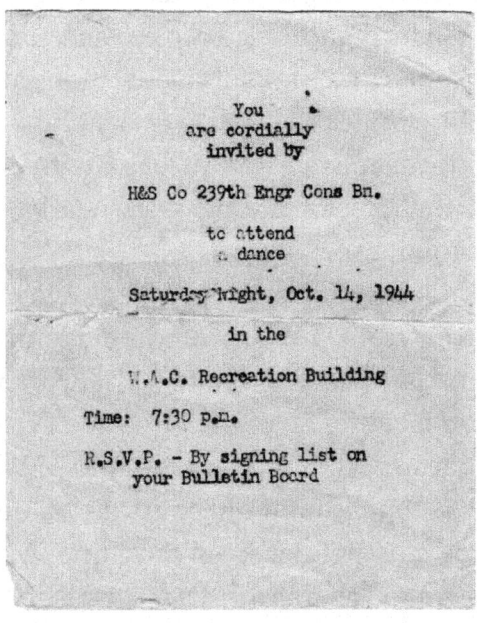

We immediately put our names on the list. I thought a dance might lift my spirits and besides the eagerness of the two GIs was contagious.

A dozen or so GIs were waiting outside the Rec building when we arrived. Whistles ensued and a couple of them jumped in front of us to open the door. There must have been more than two hundred enlisted men and a few officers already inside. There was only about 20 of us and that included a couple of Army nurses.

I recognized the song over the PA system right away. It was Peggy Lee with the Benny Goodman Band singing *Somebody Else is Taking My Place*. An area of the room had been cleared as a dance floor. A phonograph was being manned by an attentive Sergeant with an ambitious stack of 78s. "Here's a brand new tune from Bing Crosby and the Andrew Sisters, 'Don't Fence Me In.'"

Someone handed me a beer. There were so many guys around us I could hardly breathe. I turned around to see Peggy walking in with two fellow officers from the Advanced Echelon. "This one should get you out on the dance floor, *Take a Chance on Love*," another Benny Goodman song with Helen Forrest singing. GIs were grabbing WACs pulling them to the dance floor.

I felt someone staring at me. I looked past the GI who had gotten me the beer towards the back wall. Our eyes met. It was Jack. He walked towards me. We stood face to face gazing at each other oblivious to the happenings around us. I stood frozen and couldn't say a word. It seemed like an eternity before he spoke.

"Fancy meeting you here," he said.

"Jack, I don't know what to say, I thought I'd never see you again."

"Let's get out of here and go to the beach."

As we walked hand and hand, I thought about the promise I made to myself if I ever saw him again. What would I say and how would I say it? A sliver of a moon hung midway over the water. The stars were set against the darkest of skies. It seemed like a million points of light were shining down on us. Jack pointed out the Southern Cross. "You can only see that constellation in the southern hemisphere." He took me in his arms and gave me a long passionate kiss.

"Jean, I can't believe you're here," he whispered in my ear. I knew I must tell him then and there. I couldn't keep this secret any longer.

"I'm married."

He looked shocked. "I haven't seen Nick for over a year. His name is Donald Lee Nicodemus and he's a Fuel and Lubricant Supply Sergeant back in the States. I love you, Jack. I will ask him for a divorce."

Unidentified handsome Sergeant whose path crossed with Nicky's as evidenced by her photograph labeled *Guess Who.*

Chapter XV
The Rains Came

RETREAT
I STOOD RETREAT LAST NIGHT
ON A FOREIGN SHORE
AT FIRST I FELT SO FAR AWAY,
FROM HOME AND COUNTRIES DOOR
BUT WHEN I SAW OLD GLORY
MY TROUBLES DISAPPEARED
AND MY SOUL WAS AT EASE
WHEN THE BUGLE CALLS RANG CLEAR
AGAINST THE BLUE OF FOREIGN SKY
WAVING STRONG AND TRUE
SHE BROUGHT YOUR THOUGHTS CLOSE TO
HOME AND OF THINGS YOU USE TO DO
I WAS GLAD TO BE AN AMERICAN
TO SALUTE OUR FLAG SO FAIR
FOR IT MADE ME CLOSE TO HOME AND FRIENDS
TO SEE IT WAVING THERE
I STOOD RETREAT LAST NIGHT
ON A FOREIGN SHORE
BUT MY HEART WAS EVER HOMEWARD
FOR IT BROUGHT HOME RIGHT TO MY DOOR
—*PFC RUTH NEWSOME, "ALABAMA"*

Not far from General Headquarters there were three Quonset huts made of corrugated steel. They were placed side by side slightly tilting downward on a gently sloping hill, overlooking Sentani Lake. Before entering the middle hut, I noticed a large smoldering oil drum out back where a GI was carefully stirring the ashes. Peggy led us to a work area with bare rectangular metal tables. It was a quiet and calm environment. Our Captain told us that we would be working on deciphering a Japanese shipping code intercept.

Sentani Lake, Hollandia New Guinea

The concentration it took to do my work often left me with no sense of time. I volunteered for the graveyard shift which often bled into the morning shift. I've always been a night owl. I much prefer to work when my concentration was not in competition with my sweat. Besides, I don't have to worry about the night prowlers around our barracks. GIs trying to sneak a peek. A rape was reported last week on the other side of camp. Thank God for the MPs and their diligence for keeping us safe.

The days are getting hotter and muggier. It is nearly impossible to sleep in our poorly ventilated tents with this stifling heat. I'm so darn tired after my shifts, I do manage to doze off and on even with the humidity and high temperatures.

We're back to regular army unlike the freedom we were accustomed to in Brisbane. Some of the men even a few officers make it perfectly clear they don't want women in their ranks. "Go home and have babies," one of the GIs called out to me.

The women officers have it the roughest. They're often shunned by their male counterparts. At least the enlisted WACs have each other. There's only a hand full of female officers. Peggy insulates our unit by keeping us busy with Signal Intelligence work. She's a great commanding officer. Because we're in a SIGINT special unit and work long hours, we don't have to do many of the routine details like the other WACs such as cleaning the latrine and KP.

Everyone has to serve on retreat. I don't mind standing my turn at the end of the day. It gives me time to reflect on my purpose and my decision to wander so far from home.

A tepid breeze passed by as I stood at attention. Retreat was sounded over the PA system as we carefully lowered the stars and stripes. A sudden gust of wind flapped the flag sideways catching us off guard. I lunged forward as the flag headed towards the ground. I caught her just in time preventing Old Glory from being disgraced and soiled. We folded the flag in half lengthwise and then lengthways again. The triangular folding ended with the blue field of stars resting in my hands. She was not waving high overhead as a symbol for life and liberty but folded in such a way protecting her colors, weighing heavy as if privileged to carry the burdens until unfurled again at sunrise.

***

With the heat came the rains. With the rains came the sadness. It rained the morning the whole WAC complement was called together to be told of the tragedy. The night before a WAC named Genevieve had been killed in a jeep accident on a slippery and treacherous mountain road. I didn't know her but the news hit me hard as it did the others. She would be buried within 24 hours in this distant land, far away from her home. Her death brought the dangers closer to all of us. I always thought that when I died, my bones and flesh would be laid to rest in the hard earth under the high sky of West Texas.

Vivian had the day off. She was alone in her barracks when the Sergeant came in looking for someone to shine Genevieve's shoes before the burial. Later that evening, Vivian told me, "It could have been any of us. I kept shining those shoes thinking it could have been any of us."

A couple of days later, we were all called together again. It appeared that malaria was running amuck. The First Sergeant pulled out a clear tiny glass box and passed it around. Inside were four or five mosquitoes. "Those are the malaria-carrying anopheles mosquitoes. Nasty creatures. They bite at a right angle and are guaranteed to make you deathly ill if you don't take your Atabrine and protect yourself by keeping your sleeves rolled down and shirt buttoned up." Come to find out you can get a mild case even if you take all the precautions. I've been lacks about taking the Atabrine.

First thing I noticed when I got to New Guinea was how yellow everyone's skin looked. I didn't know if it would be permanent and didn't want to ruin my complexion so I stopped taking my Atabrine. That Sergeant scared the bageebees out of me. After a while you didn't even notice that everyone had skin the color of old corn.

***

It was movie night and I looked forward to seeing *National Velvet*. Posted on the WAC bulletin board was a write up about the movie. It was produced and directed by the famous Clarence Brown, starring Mickey Rooney with a young newcomer named Elizabeth Taylor. The posting gave a little description of what the movie was about. It read, "A jaded former jockey helps a young girl prepare a wild but gifted horse for England's Grand National Sweepstakes."

Jack and I had the evening off. It had been weeks since we had spent any time together. A theatre was set up outside our tent barracks with a large movie screen and outdoor projector. To get the best spots, we set our chairs out in the open area early in the morning. We marked our places by putting papers with our names under rocks.

Jack brought ice cold beer. What a treat. I asked him how he cooled them off and he said a Seabee owed him a favor. A light wind and the cold beer took the edge off the heat. A bank of clouds rolled in.

The film started at sunset. Mickey Rooney played Mi a penniless drifter and ex-jockey. We watched the lovely young Elizabeth Taylor ride Pie with grace through the British countryside. I thought of Katie and how she and Junie loved to ride horses back home.

All of a sudden, the sky opened up. The timing could not have been worse, shutting down the movie right in the middle of Velvet riding Pie in the 5 mile Grand National horse race. The rain came down so hard and so fast, we left our chairs in place and ran for cover. I don't know when I will be able to see the ending and if she won.

WACs tent barracks and outdoor theatre, Hollandia New Guinea

By the time I'm off duty again, the movie will be on its way to entertain other soldiers on another island. After the interrupted movie night, it seemed like it never stopped raining. When it wasn't raining, it was dark and gloomy or steamy and stinking hot. We were all on edge. Stories of MacArthur's advances in the Southern Philippines and his successful landings on the beaches of Leyte flooded the post. The heavy rains slowed the drive to completely secure the big island. The Japanese had moved inland and were maintaining a strong hold. One of the Aussies described it as a "bloody blood bath."

Chapter XVI
No Woman is an Island

No man is an island
Entire of itself.
Each is a piece of the continent,
A part of the main.
If a clod be washed away by the sea,
Europe is the less.
As well as if a promontory were.
As well as if a manor of thine own
Or of thine friends were.
Each man's death diminishes me,
For I am involved in mankind.
Therefore, send not to know
For whom the bell tolls,
It tolls for thee.
—John Donne, 1624

Captain Stryker, commanding officer of the 5205th, stood in her office holding her orders from General Headquarters, orders to move her detachment from Hollandia to Leyte. It had been less than 30 days since General MacArthur's forces had made the initial landing to recapture what he had lost months after Pearl Harbor.

MacArthur was criticized for not moving his Air Force out of Luzon, as instructed the morning after the devastating bombing of Pearl Harbor. Time was of the essence but MacArthur refused to act by withdrawing his fleet of B-17 bombers from eminent danger or to launch his own attack on the enemy. He believed a Japanese attack on the Philippines was "unlikely." He would soon be proven wrong.

While aircrews ate lunch, the Japanese completed their second major attack in two days. This time on Clark Field 40 miles northwest of Manila. Every plane on the field was destroyed, half of MacArthur's entire air arsenal gone, human causalities immense. A series of Japanese assaults forced the US defensive lines back.

MacArthur ordered a general retreat to Bataan Peninsula and Corregidor Island known as "The Rock." On February 22nd, 1942, MacArthur was "ordered" by President Roosevelt to leave Bataan and go to Australia. Leaving General Jonathan Wainright, the tall gaunt West Point commander behind with 11,000 soldiers to put up the gallant fight. The Battling Bastards of Bataan, the Eagles of the Rock managed to hold out until May.

Wainright was captured and took part in the Death March. American and Filipino prisoners of war were taken by the Imperial Japanese Army on a sixty-mile forced march. Starvation and brutality sent many of the soldiers, sailors, marines and civilians to their deaths.

After retreating from Bataan, MacArthur continuously lobbied the President to give him the go-ahead and resources to do what it would take to recapture the Philippines. He was determined declaring "I shall return!" It wasn't until July of 1944 that he had convenience FDR to do so. General MacArthur and Admiral Nimitz met with the President at Pearl Harbor. Admiral Nimitz wanted the assault to be further north on Formosa. At the end of the heated debate, the President approved both operations giving MacArthur the upper hand. The Commander and Chief gave his permission to go in to the Philippines first. They would shift operations further north to invade Okinawa as their advances progressed.

Captain Stryker knew of MacArthur's arrogance and his obsession to return to the Philippines as a hero. She had heard the talk from GIs and Army Nurses, who were there before and during the Japanese invasion. Stories of starvation rations and lack of supplies while the General and his staff officers, "The Bataan Gang" lived high on the hog.

What she knew for sure was that General McArthur was her Supreme Commander and he was taking back the Philippines like he promised. She had been waiting for this day. Her WACS were trained and prepared. They were ready and eager to serve. The night of November 25th, Captain Stryker departed from Sentani Airstrip. Twelve of her enlisted women from the 5205th Advance Echelon accompanied her.

This core group was selected to help set up the intercept station and the quarters for later arriving WACs. Their transport was a Douglas C-54 Skymaster, the large work horse aircraft used by the Army to carry cargo and passengers. They flew over the Pacific and the Celebes Sea, landing eight hours later on the Tacloban Airstrip at Leyte in the Southern Philippines.

On December 1st about a week after they arrived, Captain Juanita Stryker started composing her first report back to the Officers of the 5205th and the USAFFE WAC Detachments in Hollandia. She began her letter describing their new home, a parochial school formerly used by the Japanese. She detailed their new environment giving special praise to a group of 24 G.I.s.

> We are delighted to have them, and happy to know they are out of mud and foxholes which they have been in, in combat since A day. They are a nice bunch of G.I.s, very helpful in putting up shelves, uncrating, moving, fixing T bars, and doing the hundreds of little things around a house which only men can do. They are quiet and orderly. You never hear a sound from them at night — though you'd think they'd have to be noisy with big shoes on a wooden floor and going up and down steps. Don't know how long they will be here — but there is not a WAC who doesn't hope they get to stay, sleep on a cot, and rest and sit in a chair as long as they possibly can. Theirs has not been an easy life.

Their arrival had been noteworthy, so she continued her letter with a thorough description.

> The day, Nov. 26th, the first ones arrived, we were welcomed by hundreds of men running from the planes and airstrip into the foxholes, ditches and brush. It didn't take us long to catch on, and to catch up with them. That day we saw two Jap planes shot down in the distance.
>
> The first 2 nights we saw firing, search lights and Ack-ack antiaircraft fire. It was all in the distance – quite beautiful to see until on second thought you remembered that it's war and not fireworks! It was also thrilling to see searchlights pick up a Jap plane.

***

The engines sputtered before winding up. Alabama and I sat on our duffle bags with our helmets and gas masks at our feet. We had been waiting on the Sentani airstrip since 0730 and it was nearly noon. The engines quieted to a low hum. Alabama looked at her watch, "Just like the Army hurry up and wait." Captain Turner gave us a wave as she boarded the C-54. "Shouldn't be too much longer if she's getting on," Alabama said.

"Did you hear anything about our assignment," I asked?

"Same as you, only that we're going to Leyte."

"I spoke with Vivian right before she left with Captain Stryker. She didn't say much, just that Stryker was ordered to select twelve of her best and head to the Philippines."

"Hey Nicky did you ever find any boots?"

"Sergeant Smith scrounged me up a pair of men's field boots. They're way too wide. Wish I had more socks."

"Good that they found you boots. The rain will be coming soon and I heard the mud could easily get over your ankles."

I had gotten comfortable with my regular shifts and weekly movie nights with Jack. No telling when I might see him again. But I had caught the excitement of the moment. There was a buzz of anticipation among the WACs, the war was turning in our favor. We were back in the Philippines. The Bureau must have confidence in our abilities sending so many of us to Leyte.

We boarded the Skymaster. Airman Miller showed us where to store our gear and pointed to the hanging jump seats. "Have a seat, ladies" he said and left to go to the cockpit. Orange webbed jump seats stretched across each side of the concaved walls. We hung suspended in the air. The cabin was empty except for the twelve of us.

"Get as comfortable as you can," Miller told us. "We have a seven hour flight. The Lieutenant says flying over the Palau Islands shouldn't be a problem but we could take enemy fire over Leyte. Once we hit our cruising speed if nothing happens, you can move around. If we encounter any turbulence, stay seated. Prepare for takeoff."

As our four-engine aircraft roared down the runway the fuselage began to violently shake. I felt the pounding of my heart pulsing in my throat as we lifted off. Alabama touched my shoulder. "Nicky we're up. You can let go of the webbing now. Relax."

Two hours in flight and all seemed to be going fine except for the occasional turbulence bump. We were trying to catch a little shut eye but every time the plane took an air pocket I awoke thinking something's not right.

Alabama stared out the window. "Look at that water, so calm and beautiful. I can see tiny islands down there. We must be in Palau."

All of a sudden there was an explosion with the plane jerking left and dropping altitude. I screamed. A blindness over took me. Waves of fear consumed me.

"What the hell was that? Nicky, you okay?" Alabama's voice pulled me back. I looked out the window and noticed some smoke coming from an engine. One of the propellers wasn't working. I kept thinking about those WASPS test pilots back home. Two died just before I left for the Pacific, crashed in Big Springs while on a training flight. You hear all the time planes going down over here because of mechanical problems. If WASPS were dying testing planes, I knew WACS could die riding in them.

"Do you think we took a hit? Are we going to crash? I don't wanna die!

I must have sounded out of control because Alabama grabbed my shoulders and began to shake me. "Straighten up! Control yourself! For heaven's sake you're a WAC. Remember your gas mask training. Don't panic. Calm yourself down."

"Everyone all right?" I looked up and there was Airman Miller. He panned the cabin. "Don't worry ladies, lost an engine but we have 3 more. The Lieutenant is communicating, as we speak, to land on Anguar. We can get her fixed there. Hang on. The landing might be a little rough"

In a reassuring tone Alabama said, "You heard Miller, nothin' to worry about. They have it all under control."

There was an uneasy shuffling in the cabin but no one made a sound during the landing. We were all relieved to have the wheels on the ground. Hundreds of men were waiting for us to exit. The Lieutenant must have given the heads up that there were WACs on board. Every service man on that tiny island must have been standing on the runway. They met us with big smiles, whistles and cat calls. It didn't matter that we were in fatigues, hair all a muss and looking like rag a muffins. We were told there were no women on Anguar and that some of the men hadn't seen a female since before the campaign to take back the Marshall Islands.

Airmen grabbed our gear and helped us in to jeeps. As we left, we saw a GI standing on a hoist with a hand written sign that read MOVIE NIGHT.

The Island was covered in dense jungle. Our driver told us that the 81st Wildcat Division won the battle to secure the three-mile long island. It was a hard fought battle with army artillery heavily damaging much of the infrastructure left by the Japs. The Japanese occupied Anguar for several years mining the high grade phosphorus used for bombs. It's amazing what those "Can Do!" Seabees did in just two months. They fully restored the pier and runway and put up a large recreation tent with a wooden stage to boot.

Our driver took us to the Mess Hall where the cooks laid out quite a spread. Pink and white orchids were placed in the middle of the table. They were different from the larger orange hibiscus we would gather by the beach in Hollandia but just as beautiful. The delicate 5 petal sweetly scented blossoms found their way in to our hair. After dinner, the guys insisted on escorting us to movie night. My escort was Corporal Barnes from a small town in East Texas. He ushered me up on stage.

I heard the MC call my name. When he said I was from Texas the hall erupted with applause and cat calls. I could feel the heat rise in my face. I couldn't make out anyone for the bright light from the spot lit everything a blaze. But I knew from their enthusiastic response that the room was filled with boys from back home.

I'd seen *For Whom the Bell Tolls* before but I don't mind seeing it again. Gary Cooper is so handsome. I never get tired of looking at him and Ingrid Bergman is such a natural beauty. Hemingway can really tell a good story. The Spanish Civil War was a fitting backdrop for the trials and tribulations of war. The movie reminds me of how people must change due to their circumstances. You must do what you have to do during war even though back home you try to live in such a way to do no harm to anyone.

I looked up and down the seated rows into the faces of soldiers and sailors sitting all around us. Ordinary men, some just boys, staring at the screen with weary expressions. I could see it in their eyes and brows, what they had experienced in the cold hard realities of war. Men, who fought tirelessly, side by side in the Marshall Islands, here on Anguar and all over the Pacific. A band of brothers who know what happens to one happens to all, reminding me that sisters in war must stick together too no matter what.

After the movie, jeeps were waiting to take us to our quarters for the night. The officers graciously gave up their digs and slept in the enlisted barracks. The next morning we were up early, fed and back on the runway. We landed without incident as the late afternoon sun lit up the hills and jungle of Leyte.

Captain Stryker was standing on the runway when we arrived. She welcomed each and every one of us with a salute and a big hug. On December 2nd Captain Stryker completed the letter to her fellow officers and members of the 5205th describing the thrilling story.

The last twelve who arrived came with the thrilling story of having landed on an island where for a while a woman had never been. The men of our service (God bless everyone) looked at the WACs and treated them as if they were angels who had descended from heaven, instead of HBT clad girls! Each was escorted to the movie, each had to appear and be introduced on the spotlighted stage — each receiving an ovation any actress would have been thrilled by.

A few WACs are going to have to return to New Guinea. The office here is not large enough to take care of them and because they are so valuable to their sections and their work must be carried on, they will have to return in a short time. I had hoped since they were here, they could be loaned to other departments, but there's no WAC who can be spared. They haven't been told. Orders haven't been cut and I am not sure exactly who they will be at this moment. They no doubt will be disappointed – but will be able to give you firsthand information.
Captain Juanita S. Stryker
Somewhere in the Philippines
1 & 2 December 1944

Cpt. Juanita S. Stryker, photo courtesy of the Army Women's Museum Archives

5205 WAC DET
Adv. Echelon, GHQ

5 December 1944

Dear Lt. Kolokotrones,
Lt. Johnson & Lt. Zepernick:

I am enclosing a copy (handwritten — we have no typewriter — or typist) of a check sheet sent to Hq. Com.

Only three or four of the EW have two pair of field shoes. Three are absolutely necessary and whether the T/O allows it or not, in a combat area it is necessary and the EW must be supplied with them.

Mud is over our ankles — and shoes stay wet continually. There is very little sun ever, during this rainy season, so three are necessary in hopes that one or two pair can dry while the others are being worn. Morning, noon and nite the shoes have to be cleaned and at present put back on while wet — which is dreadful to feel and may lead to colds.

Be sure each EW has three pair of field shoes before she leaves for this Advanced Echelon.

Also it is necessary to have more clothing in this rainy weather. Five HBTs and shirts will not keep you in dry clothes. Issue each EW with eight of each – (HBTs or slacks – also shirts). Be sure each has eight pairs of slacks. Some of the last EW who came had only three pairs of HBTs and three pairs of socks. There is no way of keeping in dry clean clothes with that number.

As you'll see I'm requesting no more WACs be sent unless equipped with boots or galoshes — Arctic galoshes would be fine. With mud and rain it is absolutely necessary. None can be procured here. I've even tried ships but could get only three pair and they are too big.

If I remember correctly someone told me the last big shipment of WACs came from the States equipped with Arctic galoshes. If so and you could get SOS to get them — it would be wonderful.

I haven't heard any complaints about the mud and rain. All of these WACs are too thrilled to be among the first — and they know our lot is luxurious beside that of the men.

However, for health reasons we must equip them better — and those who are to come.

My best to everyone.

Juanita S. Stryker

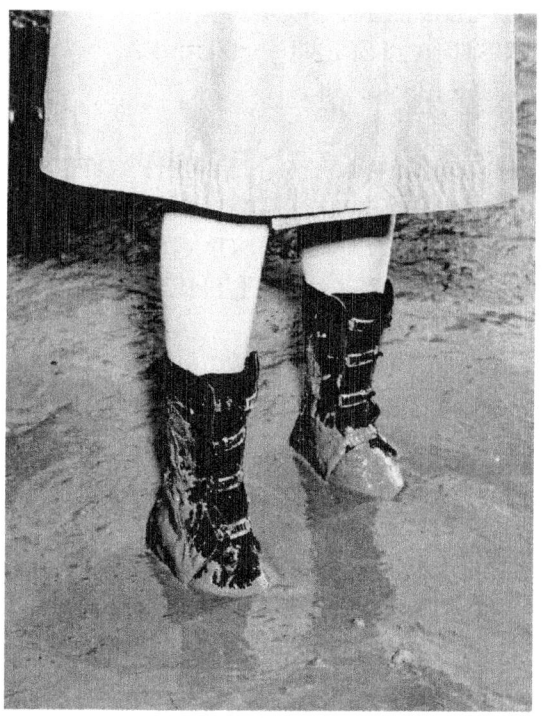

Photo from the McGraw Collection courtesy of the Army Women's Museum Archives

Chapter XVII
O're the Foam to Roam

"CHRISTMAS IN NEW GUINEA"
1944

IF I LIVE TO BE A HUNDRED
TIS TRUE I'LL NE'ER FORGET
THE CHRISTMAS I SPENT IN GUINEA
IN THE YEAR OF 44.

IT IS TRUE THEIR WAS PLENTY OF PARTIES
WITH BEER AND LIQUOR TOO
AND EVERYONE WAS DRINKING
TO TRY AND FORGET WHAT THEY USE TO DO

ON CHRISTMAS TWAS A RAINING
NOT AT ALL LIKE CHRISTMAS AT HOME
WHERE SNOW AND TREES WERE GLISTENING
AND THE CHRISTMAS CAROLS SUNG.

TIS TRUE WE MADE A CHRISTMAS TREE
WHICH WE DECORATED WITH CIGARETTES,
SOAP AND COLORED PAPER TOO.
WE BOUGHT SOME LITTLE PRESENTS
FROM THE PX IN OUR CAMP
WHICH CONSISTS OF VERY LITTLE
SUCH AS SOAP AND POWDER PUFFS.

WE HAD A CHRISTMAS DINNER
OF TURKEY AND SOME OF THE TRIMMINGS
FIXED UP AS BEST COULD BE
IN THIS FAIR COUNTRY OF NEW GUINEA

YET WE ARE ALL A HOPING
THAT CHRISTMAS OF 45
WILL SEE US AT HOME WITH OUR FAMILY'S DEAR
ALL SITTING BY THE FIRE SIDE

AND WHEN THAT DAY COMES
WE WILL ALL SIT BY THE FIRE
AND TELL OUR TALES OF GUINEA
IN THE CHRISTMAS OF 44.

—NICKY

I was delighted to receive a letter from Corky shortly after my return to Hollandia. Vivian and I had no idea where she was. I thought I would see Corky in New Guinea or Leyte. Or maybe she was still in Oro Bay but we didn't think so; most of the WACs had left there months ago.

Our unit was sent back from Leyte because there was no place for us to work. Captain Turner said what we're doing was too important to have us sit idle and we must carry on. Vivian would remain with Captain Stryker. Peggy doubted if we would return to the Southern Philippines. She said we would stay put for now. If MacArthur's campaign goes as planned the brass may have a different destination in mind for us.

The APO address on Corky's letter was from Brisbane. Around the same time I left Brisbane for New Guinea, Corky left New Guinea for Brisbane. She was working as a stenographer but due to her classification was not at liberty to say where. I envisioned her working at MacArthur Central in the building Vivian pointed out during our sightseeing.

Corky wrote that she had met an Aussie named Woodie at a pub, who knew me. *Odd looking girl, very friendly, thought the world of you. She said you worked at Central Bureau together.* Woodie gave her enough information to track me down. Corky wished me a Merry Christmas and said she often reminisced about our New York escapades.

Every outfit put up their own Christmas tree, each an original. Jungle greenery strung from tent poles and branches of bushes gathered together in traditional shapes. The security patrols dragged a couple of evergreens back to camp from the rainforest, the largest of which was set up in our mess hall. We walked from barracks to barracks caroling and taking in the decorations. C and K rations cans were hung as ornaments. Empty cans were used as shadow boxes with pictures of Santa Clauses, snow scenes and Madonnas mounted inside using Christmas cards sent from back home.

A colored unit suspended a jungle vine teepee from the ceiling of their tent. It was adorned with bright colored paper cutouts in the shapes of corn, fruits, candles and the occasional baby Jesus. I have no idea how they found those brilliant reds, yellows and blues.

I didn't mind working on Christmas Eve. Jack was on detail and I would prefer to be busy instead of pretending to be in the holiday spirit. At break we stood under a clear starry sky around a bonfire outside our Quonset hut. Someone handed me a cup of hot spice tea. In the distance we could hear the native people singing from across Sentani Lake. The lake was the most beautiful I'd seen, shimmering like silver. At first we couldn't make out the carol but soon realized it was "Silent Night." We joined in on the second chorus.

When our singing ended, we heard caroling from the opposite direction. This time it was male voices deep and rich in tone singing "Oh Holy Night."

It was raining when I got off work early Christmas morning. I was plum tired out so I immediately climbed in bed and slept until late afternoon. I dreamed of the Christmas my daddy gave me a porcelain headed baby doll. Junie was so jealous of that baby doll. "You're daddy's favorite that's why he gave you that baby doll," she told me with tears in her eyes.

I don't know why I did it and when mama asked me I just shrugged. I took a meat cleaver and started hacking at her face. I thought if I made her ugly, Junie wouldn't be so jealous of that baby doll.

I woke up feeling strangely abandoned like an orphan must feel. Alabama dragged me to Christmas dinner and I was glad she did. There were two turkeys stuffed with dressing, jelled cranberry sauce in the shape of the cans and pumpkin pie. Turkey and dressing has always been my favorite. The dressing was not near as good as Helen's but to me it was the best meal I'd eaten in the army.

A four piece band made up of GIs played Christmas music while we ate. The trumpet player announced they would be playing the New Year's Eve dance. Jack said he wouldn't get any leave until after the first of the year. I volunteered to work so one of the other girls could go to the dance.

***

Morale was downright dismal. Junior would have said, "Lower than a snakes belly in a wagon rut." It's been raining 24/7. Our tent is leaky and everything is covered in mud. We spend hours trying to dry out our socks. Thank God for the six pairs I received from Katie at Christmas. Will the monsoons ever end?

I quietly did my assignments. The tedious decrypting became wearisome and mind numbing. Instead of losing my sense of time, it dragged on. We were crawling through the intercepts. It had been forever since we made a hit. Our sense of accomplishment had faded.

"I called this meeting because I am worried about your morale." Peggy walked around her WACs as they stood at attention. "I want each of you to write two poems about your experiences while in the Pacific. What's the matter, Nicky?"

"I've never written any poetry. Don't know if I can."

"But you will or you'll have to do KP and latrine duty. That's an order."

Our Captain was the most serious I had ever seen her.

"Write about Brisbane, New Guinea, this past Christmas, how you feel. Doesn't matter what you write. Report back here in exactly 48 hours and bring your poems."

We walked into the room where she placed five chairs in a circle. "Sit down," she said. "I'll start. We'll each read a poem and round robin until were done."

Peggy lifted her paper and began.

"I DREAMED"

LAST NIGHT I DREAMED OF FLANDERS FIELD
FOR POPPIES WAVING FAIR
OF CROSS ON CROSS EACH IN IT'S PLACE
IT WAS QUIET AND PEACEFUL THERE
AND SOLDIERS LONG DEAD AND GONE
LAY SLEEPING WITHOUT CARE
LAST NIGHT I DREAMED OF FLANDERS FIELDS
OF POPPIES STAINED WITH BLOOD,
OF CROSS ON CROSS UPON THE GROUND
CRASHED SPATTERED ALL WITH MUD,
AND SOLDIERS LAY IN RESTLESS SLEEP
DISTURBED BY TANKS ABOVE
THEY GAVE A MOAN OF ANGUISH
TO THINK THEIR CAUSE WAS LOST
FOR WHICH THEY DIED, AND NOW

THEIR SEEPING BENEATH A CROSS BUT
STRONGER HEARTS AND MEN
THEIR SONS BY HERITAGE
NOW CARRIED THEIR BANNER FORWARD
TO THE END OF VICTORY,
EACH HOLDING WITHIN HIS HEART
THE RIGHT TO LIVE WITH FREEDOM
AS THEIR LIVING PART"

We didn't know if Peggy had written the deeply moving words so heavily influenced by the familiar World War I, "In Flanders Field." It didn't matter for she had shared something of herself. I was next. My poem was not as sober or thoughtful as the Captain's but I was willing and ready to share a piece of myself to my comrades in this far away land.

"My poem is called 'Why Not.'"

I suppose lots of tales have been told about Guinea
Including the tall one, "You are sure to get skinny";
But from what I've seen, I'll not tell any,
    'cause I like it here!
There may be more bugs than Carter has pills.
There may even be Japs hiding out in those hills;
But to me, it means twice as many thrills,
    'cause I like it here!
'Course it rains & rains, then it rains some more;
And there's mud and sand and dust galore.
Then we're gigged, in spite of that, for dirt on the floor,
    But I like it here!
Wearing men's pants really isn't so bad...
And Atabrine complexion is quite the fad...

And as sad sacks go, we're sadder than sad,
  And I <u>Still</u> like it here!
I'm as contented in Guinea as a dog with a bone.
I made it my choice o'er the foam to roam,
And there just ain't any way of gettin' home!
  --So <u>Why Not</u> like it here?

Something happened that afternoon as we went round the circle reading poems to each other. We laughed. We cried. It was like a fever broke. A weight was lifted. As if the rains had subsided.

Chapter XVIII
Mail Call

I wonder who's kissing her now,
I wonder who's kissing her how,
Wonder who's looking into her eyes,
Breathing sighs, telling lies;
I wonder who's buying the wine,
For lips that I used to call mine
I wonder if she ever tells him of me,
I wonder who's kissing her now.

> —"I Wonder Who's Kissing Her Now"
> *Lyrics by Will Hough and Frank Adams*

Mail call and I have two V-mails from Nick and a letter from Tommie! I'm still getting my stateside mail from an APO in San Francisco. It's getting better but sometime I have several weeks of mail show up all at once.

6 Jan, 1945
V-Mail from Sgt. Donald L. Nicodemus, Matagorda Island, Foster Field, Texas

Hello Jean,
Can't send you the papers until sometime in Feb. I haven't the money. I have met someone too.
Nick

14 Jan 45
V-Mail from Sgt. Donald L. Nicodemus Lowry Field, Colorado, Remote Control Gunnery School

Hello Jean,
Don't know if I can get the divorce here in Colorado but will try when I get the money, this is if you still want it and will sign the papers. I sure like it here a lot better than I did at the Island.
Don

PFC Tommie Edwards somewhere in the Marianas islands
January 15, 1945

Hello Sweetheart,
 How in hell are you? I received your letter a few days ago and was surely glad to know that everything is okay by you except of course the trials and tribulations of war. I hate War! Eleanor hates war! Who in the hell don't hate war, Rosie.
 I guess you are pretty well seasoned trooper by now kid: from the sound of your letter you are having it about like the rest of us. Now, honey, don't let that saying about the Air Corps having everything throw you. That applies only to tools and things to work with. Our soldiering, clothes, chow, etc. is just like everyone else's, if as good. Just don't let anyone ever fool you that we

don't know how to use our pieces or drill or hike 25 miles, either. We don't do it every day, but neither do the doughboys put in their 8 to 16 hours a day putting out the labor and the Seabees work even harder than we. All soldiers do is just soldier and everyone's pasture looks greener than your own. Since we have been here, we have lived in pup tents in the mud and crap, and we have eaten everything from C-rations to D-ration with boiled grasshoppers for desert. Our chow right now is just the same as yours only I expect you have better cooks to prepare it. And have you tried washing you're a— in a helmet yet? I have. But, as you said, we have everything, so all that rough stuff is pat. The snipers are cleaned up, we now live in Pyramidal tents (we managed for enough lumber to floor ours and build a frame), have a whatcha' call it hut for a mess hall, have mail call once a day, have a PX (such as it is), even have fur lined fox holes and luxury of luxuries – we have showers. Things are gradually shaping up and it really isn't so bad here, honey. In fact, we are on the nicest island of this group. I'm really not complaining about anything at all except the fact that the war is going on.

What job are you doing now? Still in Special Service? I surely wish it were possible for us to be on the same island. That really would be the day. How much beer do you get there? We get two cans every other day (when they have it) and hot at that. It's better than none, but wouldn't a good cold one be swell boy!

I'm glad you are getting your mail O.K. now. I hear from Dub, Mother, Kat, Helen & Ruth

I'm sure that you have heard of Dub & Kay being married. He went with her when we were in California and should have married her then, for she is certainly one swell kid. I know you will all love her.

What are you planning on after the war, or have you thought about it. You and Dub and I will have quite a credit between us, and it would be nice if we could all get into something together. Dammit, I forgot you were married. Guess that foils the partnership idea. Anyway, it was a nice thought.

Oh, I forgot to tell you that I now have my freedom again. Guess I've begun to run uncle Earnest a close second. Just ain't found the right one yet –probably never shall. Oh well, good as a change of localities?

What does the war look like from there, and what are your rumors about it being over? We never hear a damn thing worthwhile here.

I'll bet your rec hall really is nice. Sure would like to be there for one of your dances, yes ma'am. There isn't even one white girl on the island and even the Jap females are locked up.

(Section cut out by censors)

Well Sis, as you know, there isn't very much a GI can write about, so will come in for a landing for this time. Will try to write again soon and you do likewise. Excuse the writing please – I'm sitting in my truck using the steering wheel for a writing desk. Well, keep sanitary sugar –Much love to you from
Your bud, Tommie

Jack has severe joint pain, high fever and a terrible migraine. He went to the orderly room and was sent straight to the hospital. I'm not feeling well myself. I think I have a fever too and this place on my leg doesn't look good. I fell a week ago on some wooden steps. Didn't think much about it at the time but now the scrape has darkened and itches like all get out.

By the time I got to the hospital, I was running a high fever and the place on my leg was multiple shades of purples with a dark blue-grey center. I got a double diagnosis, Malaria and Jungle Rot. I wish I had been better about taking my Atabrine. The doctor said you can get Malaria even when you take the prevention. He wasn't that worried about the Malaria. It was the Jungle Rot that concerned him.

The treatments were brutal. It began with Vitamin B and C shots. They bathed my leg in some kind of potassium elixir and a liquid that smelled like camphor called Frazer's solution but the wound continued to look bad. There was talk of evacuating me to a general hospital back in the States but the doctors decided to try something new. They're using an experimental treatment that includes a medicine called penicillin. I got a triple typhoid injection along with a penicillin shot which gave me chills and a fever of over 104 degrees. The shock response was expected. It left me exhausted. I slept for days. When I woke up there was a letter from Tommie sitting on the bed stand.

PFC Tommie Edwards somewhere in the Marianas Islands

March 14, 1945

Hi Sister:

How's the soldier? Up and at 'em, I betcha. I'm feeling fine and everything is hunky dory over this way maybe it's because we had steak for dinner, boy! It would have been tough bull, at home, but over here it was delicious steak.

Guess you have been hearing about our B-29s making Mr. Toyo have nightmares. Those are the babies and I'm glad to even be hauling chow for the guys who fly 'em.

What's cooking over your way? Surely, would like to attend one of your shindigs. We ain't got no women to have one with. Well, a few nurses did come in but you can imagine who has them all served up. New Guinea must be quite a place. I hear we will soon be permitted to say which Marianas we are on. We can now say we shipped out from Seattle. Won't you be glad to be out of this and able to tend to your own business without some rank proud person having authority to chew on your a--.

Has your boyfriend recovered from the dengue? Hope so. Watch yourself kido and don't let this war time love throw you. Being away from home surroundings sometimes causes people to imagine things.

Well, I gotta go now, so will close and try again later. Keep sweet, honey and write your big bud occasionally.

Oh yes, I had a card from Pvt. Thomas E. Bizzell Jr. 38712376 Co. A - W.O.P.C. - Ft. Bliss, Texas. Imagine it. They are lousy for taking him.
   Love, Tommie

   P.S. Am enclosing a couple of snapshots taken recently.

I reread Tommie's letter. Thank God I have something positive to write him back. The docs decided not to send me to a state-side hospital. My leg is healing thanks to the injections and the remedies used for jungle rot.

Good news for Jack too. He has recovered from the dengue fever and was released today. He dropped by to see me on his way back to his unit, looking very thin. His eyes were sunken, his skin pasty and he seemed distant.

I got another letter from Nick, written over a month ago. He's in B-29 Gunnery School now. I wrote him back the day I got his V-Mail to tell him I still wanted the divorce. He says he has started the paper work but I'm not sure he's pushing it forward.

Over three weeks in the hospital and the month of March is gone. I'm released for duty with orders to wash my leg in Frazer's solution every day. I walked into my tent with a bottle of the Frazer's in hand to the surprise of colored crape paper hanging from the poles and a hand painted sign saying WELCOME BACK NICKY!

Chapter XIX
Acts of Merit

D-U-T-Y

Once upon a time, a little piece of Red, White and Blue, floated over BATAAN, in the bright sunshine of a PEACEFUL world.

Then came Pearl Harbor and the Peaceful World... vanished into the past, and OUR COLORS became stained with the blood of men women who were wounded and died...for the FREEDOM it represented; WET...with the tears of those who WAITED; AND...Trampled in the dust of a dry season; buried in the MUD of a tropical rainy season... BY... W-A-R

BATAAN... became a symbol; As BIG as the world... and the WAR. It's scope of employment knows no bounds...except...the SIZE of the SOULS...the strength...of the CHARACTER, and...the LOVE, and the FAITH, in the HEARTS...of MEN and WOMEN who do their duty.

—*Mae Murphey, 8 April 1945*

The word got out that Colonel Sinkov was arriving this afternoon. It was rare for the Commander of the Central Bureau to turn up in Hollandia. We all wanted to meet him and were anxiously waiting.

Colonel Sinkov and Captain Turner walked into our Quonset. Alabama and I were working the evening shift. He had requested that Peggy be his escort when inspecting the Signal Intelligence offices. He was an unimposing man, short in stature with a receding hair line, dressed in battle fatigues.

He strolled around the building in a relaxed manner. We immediately stood at military attention when he approached our work area. "At Ease," he said almost apologetically. To my surprise, he recognized me and called me by name. "Nicky, Peggy tells me you had a pretty rough bout with jungle rot in March. Glad to have you back." He briefly looked at our worksheets before saying, "Tomorrow we have arranged a short informal ceremony. Good work on the shipping code decipher."

Peggy smiled.

The Japanese shipping code intercept that we worked on when first arriving Hollandia had been a bonanza. We identified the location of a Japanese warship which was torpedoed and sunk by the Allies. We got a "That a girl" at the time. Captain Stryker said she would recommend us for commendations but we hadn't heard neither hide nor hair about it since, not until now.

We were waiting in the WAC Rec building with Captain Turner, when Colonel Sinkov arrived with an Army photographer. Everyone was in battle fatigues. You could not tell officers from enlisted. It was important in a battle zone that no identifying insignias be visible especially with such a high ranking officer. He handed each one of us a Letter of Commendation and said, "What you did to locate that ship is considered an act of merit and is worth more than a piece of paper. What you're doing is essential to winning this war and I will put you in for promotions and bronze stars." After the brief ceremony our letters were gathered up and delivered to our barracks.

The photographer insisted we take pictures down at the mess hall where the light was best. On our way, I walked side by side with the Colonel and took the opportunity to speak to him. "Colonel Sinkov, I'm so honored to be a part of your command."

"I'm honored to be your commander and you can call me Abe," he replied.

We reached the wooden walkway. The Colonel stood at the end of the boardwalk with the tent behind him. He motioned for Peggy and me to get on either side of him. He put his arms around our shoulders like a proud and loving father, a photograph I will always cherish. It was a great day.

L-R, Cpt. Margaret Turner, Col. Abraham Sinkov, Pvt. Billie Jean Nicodemus
Hollandia New Guinea, 1945

***

Colonel Sinkov sent a message to Peggy to meet him at the Signal Intelligence Headquarters office at 0800. She knew he was expected to leave for Clark Air Force Base later that morning. Lieutenant John R. Thomas, operations officer for the WAC detachment and Colonel Sinkov were waiting in the office when she arrived. "Peggy we're sending you and your girls to Luzon. General MacArthur is setting up an Advanced SIGINT field office at San Miguel in the Tarlac Province, not too far from Manila. You'll be the first cryptologic unit to be stationed there."

The Colonel handed her the orders. "It will not be an assignment without danger," he said. "It's mostly secure but there are still some insurgent Japs hiding out in the hills. I would suggest that you prepare your WACs for what they will see and might encounter."

The Liberation of Manila was one of the most destructive and bloodiest campaigns of the war, second only to the devastation at Warsaw. Nicky and her unit would witness the evidence of war. They would travel the same route the American armies took when advancing south from the Lingayen Gulf to drive out the Japanese on their way to liberate Manila.

Manila was truly an international city full of Asian and Western revered architecture. But now, most of these treasures were leveled by American and Japanese air attacks. What targeted and indiscriminate bombing didn't destroy, Americans armed with flame throwers, grenades, bazookas and howitzers on the ground finished the job. The "Pearl of the Orient" didn't have a chance with the intensive combat that lasted for over a month. Even after the Japanese Imperial Army retreated to the rural interior of the island, General Yamashita, resisted orders and remained in Manila with close to 10,000 of his marines. Many Filipinos were caught in the crossfire. Yamashita's exterminationist tactics massacred tens of thousands of innocent civilians.

MacArthur returned to "The Rock," days after the Japanese were defeat on Corregidor. It had taken him three years to regain what he had disgracefully lost. By early March the Bataan Peninsula, Corregidor and Manila were under his control. He planned to set up his Headquarters in Manila, but first he had to clear the city of the insurgents. There were reports of continued Japanese resistance throughout the city and countryside. He could not hesitate if they were to continue the offensive and advance on to Japan.

***

Jack wasn't the same after he got released from the hospital. Even at the V-E Day celebration, he was quiet, not his usual good-humored self. With victory in Europe, our spirits were lifted to the possibility of the same in the Pacific. But Jack just sat drinking beer, acting like he had something on his mind.

I hadn't heard a thing from him in over a week. I would be leaving soon for the Philippines so I sent a note that I needed to see him. There was a dance on Saturday night and I asked him to meet me at the Rec hall. I waited for hours, anxious for his arrival. Every time a GI walked through the door, I was overwhelmingly disappointed when it wasn't him. Something was wrong and I couldn't put my finger on it.

He walked in at the moment the tempo of the band music changed from a peppy swing to a slow foxtrot. He had a worried look on this face. "Jean lets go outside." He took my hand and we walked for about ten minutes in complete silence before he began to talk. "When this god damn war is over, I'm going back home. I'm married too. I can't do it, give up my entire family and all."

I looked in his eyes, they seemed tired and empty. Tommie warned me that something like this could happen. I felt nauseous. I walked back to my barracks and fell on my cot. I couldn't even cry. I laid there feeling rejected like I had a hole in my gut.

***

I had no time to wallow in my sorrow, by mid-week we were on our way to the Philippines. We landed at Clark Air Force Base about 40 miles from Manila.

When we got off our C-47 transport, I couldn't believe the number of B-24 bombers lined up on the airfield. They were getting ready for air strikes on Formosa.

I had seen the pin up girls painted on the noses of the fighter planes in Hollandia and Anguar but never witnessed such a display as at Clark Field. Liberators with nose art depictions representing names liked Lady Luck, Daddy's Girl and Patient Kitten. They were lined up one right after another. A nude lying on her back named Sleepy Time Gal showed real artistic talent. I thought the one of the fully clad cowgirl with stockings and a western hat was the most tasteful. Her skirt was blown up just enough to reveal her long legs. She was named appropriately Up Drafter which was lettered from the bottom up instead of the typical top down.

While some of the WACs were offended by the images, Alabama and I thought many were rather good. It seemed only fitting that pilots and crew were naming their planes after women in the tradition of sea captains naming their ships. You know what they say, boys will be boys, besides the portrayals of home, luck and desire may just provide these bronco busters the confidence they need to hang in there during rough times.

We were taken directly from the airfield by troop truck to Camp San Miguel some twenty-five miles north. We witnessed the destruction of war firsthand the entire way. It looked like tornados had hit in all directions. Overgrown and unattended rice patties and sugarcane fields were littered with wrecked planes and debris. Buildings in rubble splattered the countryside. The occasional stone steps intact leading upwards to nowhere. The walls and roofs of bombed out houses were patched with bamboo, tin and grass. The houses looked barely inhabitable.

Women wearing cone shaped straw hats with their small children walked along the side of the road. Some of the children wore wooden sandals while others were barefooted. A boy wearing only a heavily soiled t-shirt threw up his hand in the shape of a V and called out "Vic-tor-ee Joe!" He had a look of surprise when he noticed we were all women except for our driver. A huge bull like creature pulling a wooden cart blocked the road. An elderly Filipino man was guiding it across with the aid of a long stick.

Peggy told us the animal was a water buffalo called a "Casabao." "Don't let their size frighten you. They are known to be quite gentle," she said as the massive beast let out a trembling snort.

We made our way along the valley floor, approaching a grove of tall trees losing sight of the surrounding mountains. The land flattened out and in the distance we saw an enclave of thatch roofed buildings. A large two story house was directly in front with two smaller structures of similar design off to the side. The big house was of Spanish architecture and still maintained some of the luster of what must have once been a grand plantation manor. Camp San Miguel had been set up at *Hacienda Luisita*, a Spanish sugar plantation dating back to 1881.

The plantation flourished during the American era from the late ninetieth century to prewar production, supplying 20% of all the sugar used in the United States. During the Japanese occupation the plantation continued to produce sugarcane. They hoped it would help ease tensions with the Filipinos by providing the desired sweetener.

But now with the Americans back in control, McArthur had different plans for *Hacienda Luisita*. "There's camp headquarter," our driver said pointing in the direction of a Spanish Manor House. We walked on floors of refined wood planks with inlayed tile and through an archway in to a large room. Radio equipment manned with operators lined the walls.

The hacienda was not only camp headquarter but a signal radio intelligence installation. We were welcomed by the men of the 978th Signal Service Company, a Filipino-American outfit who had been at the camp for months. They were charged with setting up and operating the radio station and message center.

The men were surprised by our gender. We must have answered the question at least ten times. What are you doing here? They were expecting the first cryptology unit to be Australian and to be men.

Chapter XX
Of Age in the Philippines

"By your dust, and by the dust of all the generations, I promise to continue, I promise to preserve! The jungle may advance, the bombs may fall again—but while I live, you live—and this dear city of our affections shall rise again—if only in my song! To remember and to sing: that is my vocation..."
— *Nick Joaquin*

Flying roaches and the abominable heat left me queasy and light headed. I sat on the edge of my bunk with my head between my legs watching a line of ants march across the floor. We are living in a squad tent until the Army finishes construction of our barracks. I'm not sure if our new living quarters will be any better given its location in an unshaded area close to a grove of trees.

General MacArthur decided to relocate most of the Central Bureau to our camp to be closer to his General Headquarters in Manila. Key punch machines, tabulators and sorters arrived yesterday. It was old home week, several of the operators we knew in Brisbane came with the equipment.

Understandably, there was no leave for my 21st birthday. The red flares high in the sky and rapid gun fire in the distance were daily reminders that enemy activity was all around. We were tightly restricted to camp. I was hoping to get a day's leave to go into the small town of San Miguel to celebrate. Maybe I'll get some of that fried chicken in one of the Filipino cafes everybody's talkin' about. No packages or letters from home either, my mail hasn't caught up with me. I worked a double shift and didn't mention to anyone that it was my birthday. There was no shortage of work to keep us busy and distract us from the threats. Filipino and American patrols were bringing in Jap intercepts which needed to be deciphered. Now that the machine department was all set up, we are expecting a WAC Signal Intelligence attachment at any time.

Tank trucks brought in water. There were no working wells on the plantation. Most days we were allowed to take a brief shower but laundry was another matter. It wasn't long after our arrival that the Filipinos from town started showing up. I walked up to a small group of women squatting in a circle when an overly anxious man caught my attention. "I wash, I sew," he said waving his arms in the air. Several of my shirts were torn and I heard that the Filipinos were very good with a needle.

"My name Datu," he said. He barely came to my chest and was very thin. I'm guessing he was probably twice my age by his creased face and protruding cheek bones. His English although broken was understandable. We settled on a price. He said his wife would do the laundry and he could sew anything I wanted and make it "fit good."

I was lucky, my clothes came back clean and pressed. The repairs were flawless. Some of the others said their clothes looked clean but had a funny smell as if the military soap given to do the laundry wasn't used. We all wondered if they didn't use our soap, what did they use?

***

Alabama and I took our time walking to the plantation house used as the SIGINT office. The early evening breeze was beginning to take the edge off the heat of the day. I was drowsy and hadn't fully woken from the few hours of sleep I tried to catch that afternoon.

We call our barracks "the oven" because of the corrugated tin roof and siding trapping the heat. I swear you could bake bread in there. The air smelled like rain. Huge drops began to fall. I could hear them plopping on the magnolia leaves nearby.

"What was that?" Alabama whispered. She was looking out towards the tall field of grass along the edge of the camp. We sped up our pace. It was in the back of our minds, what we had heard that morning in the mess hall. A GI had let it slip. Filipino guerillas had identified a small band of Japs hiding out close by.

I was getting ready to send a routine message by teletype when the teleprinter next to me spit out a communication from General Head-quarters. Alabama was receiving instructions from Lora, when we heard the deafening explosion and felt the shock wave. "Grenade!" Alabama yelled as we hit the floor.

***

News of the attack spread like wildfire throughout the camp. Captain Turner was headed to Camp Headquarters when she encountered the two MPs. She had planned to check on her girls later that evening. The Major was expecting a teletype of importance from Headquarters. When she heard of the attack, Peggy bee lined towards the SIGINT office with the two Military Police.

"Wait a minute, Captain," the tall MP said thrusting his arm in front of her. They stopped and listened. All was quiet so they decided to continue. They approached the front of the SIGINT building, everything seemed secured. The MP gave a firm one two knock on the door.

No one answered so Peggy yelled, "Open the door!"

They heard the bolt unlatch and the door open. Nicky looked at Peggy. Nicky's face held no color as if she was in shock. Peggy said her name and she stepped backwards to reveal Alabama who was clutching the revolver pointing it directly at her Captain.

Peggy held out an open hand and Alabama released the trigger and placed the gun in her palm. The coldness of the metal sent a chill up her spine. She placed it back on the table beside the door. Peggy looked around the room noticing a half dozen stunned

SISers and a young MP standing at attention holding a M1.

"We got those Japs ma'am, all five of them, no prisoners, two behind the building; 5th infantry got the other three back in the jungle." Just checking to make sure all is okay in here."

"Thanks Corporal, We'll handle it now."

The Corporal left through a kicked in door at the back of the room. "I'll get engineering to fix this right away," he said as he faded away in to the darkness.

"I think you gals have had enough excitement tonight, go get some rest and report back here for your shift tomorrow. I'll stay until your replacements report."

Hands shaking, Nicky handed Captain Turner the crumbled teletype. She unfolded the paper and noticed right away it was the *Ultra* message the Major was waiting for.

***

The next morning Alabama and I decided to go to chapel. Hired by the Army, the Filipinos had built a lovely church. The thatched building with twin gabled roof and a tall steeple had a large bamboo cross sitting on top. We walked in to God's house hoping to find solace and the confidence to carry on. The choir was made up of mostly WACs and a few GIs. Their voices rose as we made our way to the hard wooden benches. The Chaplain spoke of faith in God and trust in our mission. The hymns uplifted our spirits.

Not long after the assault on the SIGINT building, I got my first 3 day pass to go to Manila for R&R. Delma Ray is stationed in Manila so I looked him up. It's been two years since I've seen him.

Delma Ray looked the same. He greeted me with that big smile of his and hugged me so tight he lifted me off the ground. It always surprises me how strong those Bizzell boys are given their size. "I have an idea, Jeanie. There's a military photographer around the corner. Let's get our picture taken together and send it home."

Delma Ray and I were dressed in battle fatigues. The photographer had a backdrop and lights on movable stands. I told Delma Ray, I wasn't dressed for such a professional photo when he started goofing around. He grabbed a sailor cap and put it on my head. "Wait a minute," I said heading to the dressing room. I brushed my hair into pigtails and placed the cap back on. We had great fun pretending we were Daisy Mae and Li'l Abner. I hadn't laughed so hard in years. Delma Ray is so handsome with his thick dark wavy hair and mischievous expression. He made a good Li'l Abner. I wasn't a half bad Daisy Mae.

Billie Jean Nicodemus and Delma Ray Bizzell, Manila 1945

"Let's go dancing. I know just the place," he told me as we left the studio. We walked along the harbor making plans for the evening when Delma Ray noticed a couple of Marines. "Look at those two, Jeanie. They look like Navajo. I betcha they're some of those code-talkers, let's go talk to 'em. "

"I don't know, Delma Ray. I have to be careful, what they're doing is top secret, we could get in trouble asking them questions."

By the time we got over their way, the two Marines had jumped into a jeep and were heading down the road. "Did you know that the Choctaw were the first code-talkers back in World War 1?" he said. I could see Delma Ray was disappointed as they drove off.

Delma Ray's grandmother was Choctaw. It had been hard for the Bizzell family at times being part Indian given the sentiments out in West Texas. The code-talkers were famous back at Signal Intelligence especially since Iwo Jima. They encoded over 800 transmissions in their native language with perfect accuracy in the first 48 hours of the battle. I would have liked to have meet them too.

I found temporary quarters at the WACs barracks on Azcarraga Street. Delma Ray dropped me off and said he would come back at 1900 hours to pick me up to go dancing.

He showed up exactly on time. Dressed in our summer uniforms, we were ready to kick up our heels. I knew something was up from the way Delma Ray was smiling at me. I followed him to the street. A brightly painted pony cart with a fringed canopy was waiting for us.

"Where to GI?" asked the Filipino driver.

I was stunned by the destruction. The streets were clear but most of the buildings were bombed out, many in rubble. We pulled up to an old two story house spared from the shelling. Music seeped out of the place. The first level of the converted night club was completely open to the street. Little kerosene lamps sat on the floor and paper lanterns hung from the rafters. Servicemen coupled with Asian beauties stood around.

"The band upstairs plays western swing," Delma Ray said.

The upstairs had a tall ceiling and foldout walls. It was amazingly cool with the circulating air. Little café tables draped in white cloths each with the same little kerosene lamps that dotted the floor. We grabbed a table. A four piece Filipino band was up on a small stage next to the dance floor. They were dressed in makeshift cowboy outfits. The guitar player wore a shiny green silk western shirt.

I felt under dressed. Other WACs in the room were in dresses or A-line skirts perfect for dancing. I didn't know I could wear civilian clothes in Manila. I asked one of the girls and she said, "Oh yes, only while off duty." I'll have to get Datu to whip me up something for next time.

Delma Ray pulled me to the dance floor. He leaned over to the band and made his request. Boy those Bizzells can dance. They take you this way and that without you even knowing where you've been or where you're going.

"I've got my eye on a girl back home," Delma Ray said. "When I get back, I'm gonna try my hand at cotton farmin' on that little piece of land daddy gave me out Stanton way. Guess you'll be hitching up with Nick wherever he's stationed after this war."

"I've asked Nick for a divorce." I'm sure everyone back home already knows so I felt it was alright to tell Delma Ray. Just couldn't bring myself to tell him about Jack.

My last day of leave, I met up with Corky. Once I got to San Miguel, she was easy to find, stationed right in Manila at General Headquarters. She was at MacArthur Central working as a stenographer the same time I was in New Guinea.

Corky wanted to show me prominent buildings that had once graced the city. She took me to see City Hall, the Legislative Building and the YMCA. They laid in ruins. The Finance Building was the worst. It had been one of the last pockets of the Japanese resistance. Blacken from the burnings, a shadow of what it had once been.

The bombed out buildings reminded me of my own shattered heart. I broke down in front of St. John's Episcopal Church. The cathedral was a skeleton of its former existence. The crumbled walls and lifeless trees left me without hope. I couldn't hold back my tears any longer. Corky was the only one who truly knew how I felt about Jack. I told her everything.

Corky held her friend's weeping body in her arms. "Nicky you're strong. You've had a love you will always remember. You may never love that way again but you will love again."

Chapter XXI
The Trinity

HOLY SONNET XIV

Batter my heart, three-person'd God; for you
As yet but knock; breath, shine, and seek to mend;
That I may rise, and stand, o'erthrow me, and bend
Your force, to break, blow, burn, and make me new.
I, like an usurp'd town, to another due,
Labour to admit you, but O, to no end.
Reason, your viceroy in, me should defend,
But is captive, and proves weak or untrue.
Yet dearly I love you, and would be loved fain,
But am betroth'd unto your enemy;
Divorce me, untie, or break that knot again,
Take me to you, imprison me, for I,
Except you enthrall me, never shall be free,
Nor ever chaste, except you ravish me.
    —*Holy Sonnets (Trinity Mediations)*
      by John Donne, 1609-1610

I tried to keep to myself on the ride back to camp. A PFC sitting next to me did his best to strike up a conversation. He asked if I had a good time on R & R but I could only respond to his questions in one word answers. I didn't mean to be rude but had a lot on my mind. I kept thinking about Nick's last letter and how he didn't say anything about the divorce papers. He mentioned that his math course for gunnery school was tough and even though he didn't say so, I got the impression he was worried about washing out. I wrote him back straight away telling him not to get discouraged and give up on his dream of being a gunner. I told him I still wanted the divorce.

Life without Jack weighs heavy on my mind. What am I gonna do after this war? Tommie wants to go into business together but I have no idea what that might be. I could apply to the University of Texas and go to college on Uncle Sam. I can't go back to the life I had before. When will this war end? We believe our work is making a difference. We will win this war but when? The Japanese are so damn unyielding.

I got back in time for mail call and received a letter from Nick. It was dated the 9th and must have gotten here in record time, only a week after he had written it.

July 9, 1945

Dear Jean,

I have received two letters from you in the last three weeks. So I will surprise you and answer. I am not having any luck on our divorce as I guess you know. It cost me damn near everything I have made and still no results.

As you can see I am in Florida now. I finish my training here the 21st. Then I get a delay in route to P.O.E. I might be seeing you in about 2 months. I am now a Ring gunner on the B-29, but don't have no idea where that will send me.

I have a swell crew. I am 6 yrs. older than anyone of them, so they all call me pop even my pilot. Gee you should see our ship. Boy is it swell and really big.

Hun I don't know what my address will be after the 26th. So just write here till I send you a change in address card.

Well honey I will close now. So don't be any meaner than your old man.

So long, Nick

***

As Billie Jean received her evening assignment, unbeknownst to her or any of her co-workers, something was about to happen that would change the war and mankind forever. Half a world away on the exact spot she had gazed upon three years prior while sitting atop a mound of gypsum, a chain reaction of gigantic proportions was about to be set in motion.

July 16, 1945, the predawn stillness at the Trinity site on the White Sands Proving Grounds would soon lay in contrast to a release of energy never seen before at the hand of man. Sitting aloft a 100-foot steel tower, an implosive plutonium device encased in a sphere of metal covered in a swarm of wiring and detonator boxes, "The Gadget" was awaiting its fate. Within seconds, a huge fireball would be released on the peaceful desert, an inferno that would rival the depths of Hell.

The First Atomic bomb, "The Gadget, Trinity Site, July 16, 1945
***

I was on duty August 6th when the teletype arrived. HIROSHIMA BOMBED. We received the message minutes after detonation. We were instructed to send the top secret communication without delay to MacArthur Headquarters in Manila. We did not know much only that a bomb code-named "Little Boy" was dropped from the Enola Gay, a B-29 bomber on Hiroshima, Japan at 08.16 hours. Rumors started circulating with every consequent report. This bomb was different. There were accounts of massive destruction from the initial explosion and ensuing fires. A huge number of causalities was expected.

Later, we learned it was an atom bomb made from uranium. Every time the bomb was mentioned Alabama got visibly upset. It seemed to bother her more than anyone. We all hoped such a powerful bomb would end the war.

Three days after Hiroshima, we received another teletype announcing a second atom bomb named "Fat Man" had been dropped on Nagasaki. This bomb was made from plutonium and was expected to be even more powerful than "Little Boy." Spirits were high that the war would end very soon.

The day after Nagasaki, Emperor Hirohito personally accepted the Allies terms of ending the war which had been rejected 17 days before. He addressed his people by radio on August 15th announcing the surrender of the Empire of Japan. On September 2nd, the Japanese Instrument of Surrender was signed aboard the battleship *USS Missouri*. The war was over.

***

Sgt. Donald L. Nicodemus
Buckingham AAF, Florida
Aug 14, 1945

Dear Jean,

Honey your letter finely caught up with me yesterday, so I will get busy and answer it. Sure hope that you get to come home now that the war is over. Boy is everyone going nuts here tonight but as for me I have stop drinking so I am not doing much. I just got off furlough last Saturday and I didn't have a drink while I was on it.

I was to ship out of here Thursday but since it is all over I don't think I will be leaving. So just write me at this address if you don't get a change of address card in a day or so.

Jean I went to see another Lawyer when I was home and she took me to a judge and they said wasn't a chance of us getting a divorce till you get back. That is if we still want one then.

Well honey I will close now. So be good and write soon.

Always, Nick

Tinian, Marianas
Sept 3, 1945

Hello Sugar;

 Received your nice letter, and to say I was glad is putting it mildly. Glad, too, to hear that everything is going nicely for you.
 Yes, sis, it's really wonderful that the old conflict is ended. V.J. Day yesterday, V.J. Day — that sounds very nice — doesn't it? I expect we are all pretty happy. Me — I'm doubly so. Only today, they announced that 35-year-olds and older would soon be released from service. That's an invigorating idea — means your big bud will probably eat some of Mom's biscuits for Xmas dinner. Good — Good. Now, if only you can make it, too — It really will be swell to be home again, eh Pimko?

And yes, it still goes about us going into business — if you still want to, that is. I hardly expect that Dub will want to join us, now that he is married. More than likely, he and Kay will head right for California. I'd like to use the old priority on G.I. surplus goods to purchase a few jeeps—to start a jeep rental service. What would you think of that for a starter — while were deciding what we'd really like to get into? If it didn't work so well (which I think it would, for a while), we could change the bodies and call 'em "jeep taxis." Or we could always sell them. I'd sort of like to try them in Okie City at first — because there is someone there who would kinda finance us — you know. I'd also thought of using the G.I. Bill of Rights equity to take a good commercial course in photography. It should be a real business for a long long time. It's just a thought. Probably will end up with a café—beer joint or liquor store. Do you have any idea — and are you still interested. Let me know — and I will know what to count on. I'm sure we could make it in almost anything. Or perhaps you have some plans for matrimony right away or something. I know I'm not wanting to settle down right away. Sort of got to get the wanderlust feeling sated. Somehow, I had sort of figured you felt the same way. Anyway, I'll wait until you get home before getting into anything — that is — if you don't beat me there.

It must be pretty nice there on Luzon. At least it is more than a five mile by twelve hunk of coral. "The Rock," they call it. "Rock happy" they call us. It's better than some tho: I guess. There's no "poison" at all here (except that issued by the brass). Quite a few nurses here now — but, you know how that goes. No Wacs or Waves, yet. They're all on Guam — headquarters.

The Beaumont gals were O.K, the last I heard. Dub hasn't written me in a couple of months. Heard from Mother the other day. They're fine Sugar, Grandmas' address is still Gen. Del. Roby, Texas. I know the little ole lady would be tickled to hear from you.

We must be having about the same type weather that you are. There really are some lovely nights here though —— occasionally. I suppose we have made it as well as guys without whiskey or romance. Could have, we have had it easy, compared to some. But, I'm ready, like you to go home — just anytime now — that they'll let me.

No honey, I can't quite picture a family of natives in a jeep — escorting the daughter on a date with a G.I. Well, it's one way to keep the G I on the level. That ain't for me though.

Well kiddo — no news from here — so — so long for now. Write soon.

Always — as ever
Your bud & buddy, Tommie

"Tinian, that's where the B 29s carrying Little Boy and Fat Man lifted off," Alabama said when I told her where Tommie was stationed. "What was your brother doing there?"

"Supply Sergeant," I told her. Alabama and I were together when the taped radio message from President Truman played over the intercom. "*We have used it in order to shorten the agony of war, in order to save the lives of thousands and thousands of young Americans.*"

I believed what our President said but I could tell Alabama was conflicted. "I'm not sure we needed to drop the second one. Why didn't they just wait a little while longer," she said. I couldn't dwell on the horrific destruction and loss of human life. The A-Bombs had ended the war. I was going home!

Chapter XXII Badge of Honor

Prayer to Athena
grey-eyed Athena, beautiful goddess,
your children are in pain.

rally us with your battle cry,
let the deaths not be in vain.

bless us with your wisdom,
the power to do what's right.

protect your sweet America,
hear our cries in the night

grey-eyed Athena, beautiful goddess,
your children are in pain.

we shall rise up and be victorious,
and live to love again.

—*Aurora McAdams*

August 26, 1945, I received special orders announcing my appointment to Technician 5th Grade. The promotion promised back in May from Colonel Sinkov. While we played the Army waiting game to go home, Alabama and I arranged a full week's leave.

We decided to go to Brisbane to properly celebrate the end of the war, our promotions and my belated 21st birthday.

Our timing was perfect. We arrived on September 15th, the day of the Victory Parade. Queen Street was lined with jubilant Aussies. Bobbies were poised every 50 feet to keep the peace. The tops of their pointed white helmets were visible as we made our way through the crowded sidewalks. We managed to find a spot on the corner down from *Manahans*.

Victory Parade, Brisbane Australia, September 15, 1945, Photo Courtesy of the Family of Vivian Paruta

A barrage of military units marched in unison one after another. I noticed a WAAAF formation and someone I thought looked like Woodie. I jumped up and down screaming her name but she looked forward never altering her gaze. Her attention never wavered. The precision of the unit was impressive.

The city was one big street party. Wild and happy Australians celebrated all day and all night. Every time Alabama mentioned we were celebrating my 21st birthday, an Aussie or GI stepped up to buy us drinks or to steal a kiss. It was all in fun. I felt free and alive. I knew I wouldn't be 21 forever. I glanced up at the Regent Portrait Studio sign and knew exactly what to do. I would capture the moment in time.

**

I gingerly placed my uniform on the sofa in the dressing room admiring Datu's handy work. The Americans were keeping Datu busy. So busy that he was able to set up shop in San Miguel. When I went into town to pick up my uniform to make sure it, "fit good," I was surprised at the perfection of his alternations. It fit like a glove accenting my slim figure.

Before dressing in my formal uniform for the photo session, I fingered the newly sewed patches on the upper left sleeve. First I felt the two stripes and T signifying my new rank. Directly above my rank was a round patch of significant importance, the U.S. Army Forces Pacific Ocean Areas insignia.

The insignia had been mindfully designed with three constellations, the North Star, Big Dipper and Southern Cross surrounding a western pointing red arrow set in a sea of royal blue. The constellations denoted the locations of the Command Headquarters. The stars served as a reminder of the single most important date to the men and women who wore it. A total of 12 stars represented the month of December, the seven stars of the Big Dipper, the 7th day and the four stars of the Southern Cross plus the North Star, the year 41.

I carefully attached my bars above the left jacket pocket paying special attention to the ones indicating the Victory and Liberation medals. I held the Pallas Athena pin in my fingers.

The symbol had more meaning now than the day Lt. Reed handed it to me at Fort Oglethorpe. Before fastening it to my collar, I thought of the myth of Athena, springing full grown and dressed in armor from the forehead of Zeus. Pallas Athena was the crusader for the use of intellect, strategy and just warfare when facing your enemies. The helmeted goddess exemplified the women I've served with every day over the past year. "I will wear her as a badge of honor," I said under her breath.

***

The photographer rearranged the lighting in hopes to capture her glow. He rarely had the opportunity to shoot such a fine looking American. She held a posture of confidence and a self-assured smile. He trusted he could seize her spirit.

She walked out for her second sitting, dressed in an elegant black chiffon dress with sheer striped sleeves.

He could hardly believe it was the same young WAC. Her garrison cap discarded for a glamorous up do. If he got the lighting just right he could highlight the finger curls on her crown and the alluring translucence of her face.

PART FOUR

Home Coming

Chapter XXIII
There is No Place Like Home

Vivian was the first to get her orders. On October 1st she boarded the *Evangeline* with 1500 others to make the crossing. Vivian, Corky and I met up one last time before she left. "I've decided to go to Japan for the occupation," Corky said.

"What for?" I asked. I couldn't imagine she didn't want to go home.

"I like the work at headquarters and they've offered me a promotion if I go."

Alabama and I received our orders on October 20th. We will go home the way we came on the SS *Lurline*. If all goes well I'll get back before Christmas.

I sat on my duffle at the Port of Brisbane waiting to board when a Monarch lit on my arm. "Where are your mates, little Wanderer?" I asked my companion. I like the Australian name for the migrating butterfly and feel a kinship to the beautiful black and orange delicate winged creature. I recalled its remarkable life cycle, dramatic changes from within, breaking out of a cocoon to emerge into an ever changing world. I too had wandered to this faraway place with a multitude of others in search of who knows what. I wonder if I can retrace my route, return to where I have come and fly without my mates like my little friend.

We sailed under the Golden Gate Bridge. It seemed like I had passed this way only yesterday yet I felt years older. I looked eastward across the bay yearning for Texas. We were sent to Stoneman Camp for staging where I was put on a train for Fort Sam Houston.

I've been at Sam Houston for over a week waiting for my release. Thursday was Thanksgiving, hopefully my last Army turkey dinner. I have all this time with nothing to do. I'm constantly thinking about my future and situation with Nick. I decided to fill out an application for the University of Texas. Leave my options open.

Katie came up to see me from Beaumont. She said the future was in oil and gas and she thought I should try and get a degree in Petroleum Engineering. I always thought if I went to college I would probably end up a teacher. Studying something technical never crossed my mind until now. It makes sense given my Army experience. I sent letters to Colonel Sinkov and Captain Turner asking them to write me recommendations.

***

I looked out the window as the train pulled up to the station. I fell in love immediately. His pale blue eyes and apple cheeks warmed my heart. The dimple planted on the left side of his face was the same as mine. The mark of an Edwards told of our relations. Luke Griffin wiggled in his grandmother's arms as the train came to a complete stop. Jo Ann stood beside them.

Tommie met me at the steps and helped me down. "How about a kiss for your big bud," he said. I suspected the Band-Aid on his nose and bruise on his cheek bone meant he had been in a bar brawl. Dub confirmed my suspicions with his bandaged right hand. "What's going on there," I said pointing to the bruise on Tommie's face.

"Too much fun I guess," he said with a shrug. Dub and Kay made a handsome couple. Dub with his pencil mustache and dashing good-looks and Kay with her dark features, light skin and petite figure.

Dub placed his arm around his new wife's waist giving her a squeeze. "Jeanie, this is Kay."

Kay looked up at Jean with a smile and said, "All these two can talk about is their little sis coming home. I'm so happy to finally meet you."

June was there holding little Bo. Jimmie Dale was holding on to her skirt. He must have grown half a foot since I last saw him. He was wearing the same cowboy hat. It sat on top of his head this time with his eyes in perfect view. Junie's rounded belly announced her third was on the way. Jo Ann stepped towards me. She looked as beautiful as ever but had a distracted wildness in her eyes.

"Where's Jimmie," I asked? She ignored my question and said, "Dub said we're all going out on the town to celebrate your coming home tonight!"

Mama heard me and said he was at college. "Got a full football scholarship."

Just as Jo Ann had said, Dub insisted on going out that night. I told him I was exhausted but he was persistent. I felt like a deer in the head lights all evening, stunned by all the commotion. Dub and Tommie took us to a private club in Midland so we didn't have to go to one of the honky tonks in Odessa.

"Gets a little rough over there in Odessa and we have the bruises to prove it," Tommie said glancing over at Dub. The celebration peeked by the second night. Alcohol was flowing like water. Dub ordered a bottle of Tequila, announcing that Kay and he were leaving for California in a couple of days. All the dancing and laughing reminded me of the time I spent with Delma Ray in Manila.

"Sure wish Delma Ray was here," I said.

"Me too," replied Junie

"Jeanie, what are you planning to do now that you're out of the Army," asked Tommie? I told him about applying to the University in Austin. "That makes sense kiddo. You are the smartest of the bunch." He didn't seem disappointed at all about me not going into business with him. "I'm going to Oklahoma City. I've put in for those surplus Jeeps, will start that taxi service I told you about. Looks like both of us will get something out of Uncle Sam."

JoAnn, Junie, Dub, Billie Jean, Tommie and Kay, Midland TX, Dec. 1945"

***

Keeping Luke away from the Christmas tree was quite a task. He could crawl faster than I could run. I thought shouldn't a sixteen-month-old be walking by now. When I grabbed him he would giggle. We really hit it off. I asked mama about the walking. She said his foot turned in and the doctor said to put him in high top shoes. I couldn't help but notice he was bow legged too. All week we practiced his walkin'. He would hold my hand and toddle around the house.

Nick called me on Christmas Eve. "I'm not going to get leave for at least a month. Do you still want the divorce?" I told him I did and that I was thinking about going to college.

"I thought things might be different with the war over and all." His voice was tender and sad. "Let's not do anything until I come see you."

Tommie decided not to leave for Roby until after Christmas dinner. When Mama pressed him about leaving earlier to see his own mother and sister Ruth, he kissed her on the cheek. "I'm not missing those biscuits of yours," he told her.

Tommie looked over at me and said, "Why so gloomy, sis?"

I didn't know if it was Tommie leaving, Nick's call or the tenth anniversary of losing BJ but I felt alone and abandoned.

"Let's go for a walk," he said.

Who knows when I will see Tommie again and a walk might help clear my head. We grabbed our coats and walked along the empty downtown streets under the grey skies. "Look at that," he said pointing to a ray of light shining through a gap between two buildings.

"See everything is going to be all right, Jeanie. Remember, you come from good stock and it helps to have your feet planted firmly on the ground so the wind don't knock you over."

Chapter XXIV
The Yellow Rose of Texas
February 1946

The Eyes of Texas are upon you
All the live long day.
The Eyes of Texas are upon you
You cannot get away.
Do not think you can escape them
At night or early in the morn-
The Eyes of Texas are upon you
'Till Gabriel blows his horn"
    —*John Sinclair, "The Eyes of Texas,"*
   Alma Mater, University of Texas at Austin

Billie Jean caught her balance. A thin layer of powdery snow covered the porch. She turned to face the door and noticed a white envelope peeking out from the top of the mail box. As she lifted the letter, her eye caught the university seal on the return address. A chill moved through her body as she stood in the cold staring at the envelope. She didn't know whether to open it right then and there or go inside to the warmth of the house. She chose the latter.

 It took her several minutes to absorb the meaning of the formal correspondence. She had been admitted to the University of Texas for the spring semester with acceptance to the College of Engineering and the opportunity to study Petroleum Engineering.

She had anticipated this moment and was surprised by her overwhelming feeling of apprehension. Nick called her on Valentine's Day. He would be getting leave soon and said he expected to have good news to share. She decided not to tell him of her acceptance to college and didn't know why she had kept it from him.

***

The metal bed next to mine was vacant, a naked mattress waited for my expected roommate. I carefully made my dorm room bed military style with all the corners perfectly folded and tucked. I sat in the middle with my legs crossed and looked at my schedule. My first class was only two days away.

The phone in the hall rang. After the fourth ring I decided to answer it. "Jean?" It was Nick. "I'm in Midland."

Nick had driven through the night in hopes to see me first thing in the morning. But instead he was on the phone at mama's house 300 miles away.

"Jean, I need to see you." We settled on meeting at noon the next day so Nick could get some sleep before heading down to Austin. He sounded hopeful.

I know he doesn't want a divorce. But what do I want? My roommate never showed. The room felt empty and deserted. I couldn't sleep. I kept thinking about my situation, over and over. As hard as I try, I can't sort out my feelings for Nick.

I'm not the same girl I was when I married Nick. I'm not the same girl I was at Fort Oglethorpe or at the Battalion dance when Jack showed up. I've crossed the Pacific, seen a larger part of the world but what does it mean now? Why does Texas have such a hold on me?

Should I take this opportunity for an education? Four years is such a long time. Should I abandon this dream to follow Nick? And what about having a family? The longer she remained awake the more questions flooded her mind. It was early morning before she got to sleep. Three hours later the alarm went off.

***

The tower chimes were ringing out "The Eyes of Texas" as she climbed the steps to go into the building. She had learned the words to the University's anthem as a child and had never liked them.

The Eyes of Texas are upon you
You cannot get away.
Do not think that you can escape them
At night or early in the morn-

Even though it didn't make sense, she felt the song wanted to control her. She felt the Eyes of Texas had drawn her home. "The Yellow Rose of Texas" had always been her favorite. She sang the preferred tune and lyrics to get the other out of her head.

"There's a yellow rose in Texas, that I am going to see,
No other soldier knows her, no soldier only me
She cried so when I left her it like to broke my heart,
And if I ever find her, we nevermore will part.
She's the sweetest little rose bud this soldier ever knew,
Her eyes are bright as diamonds they sparkle like the dew;
You may talk about your Clementine, and sing of Rosa Lee,
But the Yellow Rose of Texas is the only girl for me."

She entered the elevator to take the 28 stories to the observation deck, their meeting place. As the elevator door opened, she saw Nick. He was looking out across the south mall towards the Capital. She could see a glimpse of the noonday sun reflecting off the dome in the far distance. He turned around at the exact moment the bell began to strike. They stood only a few feet apart looking at each other as the chimes clicked off twelve times.

He seemed to sense a great distance between them, immense like the ocean that had separated them for so long. He moved forward and flashed her that grin of his. "Jean, I have orders for Europe!" He was waving the paper in the air. "Come to Germany with me."

AUTHOR'S NOTES
About The Writing of This Book

This book is based on the life of my mother Billie Jean Edwards Nicodemus, who served as a WWII Signal Intelligence Service WAC in a select cryptologic field unit in the Southwest Pacific under General McArthur.

The heart of her inspired story is drawn from her memories and personal stories. Documents found at her death to include letters, military orders, V-Mails, photographs, poems, magazine/newspaper articles and a written memorable experience provide the substance. Historical research helped to shape its content.

I contacted family members to collect additional stories and to confirm those I had heard from my mother. Women who served as Navy and Army WWII cryptographers were interviewed. The family of Vivian Paruta, a fellow WAC who befriended my mother at Fort Dix and also served in the Asiatic Pacific, shared valuable photos and a personal memoir written by their aunt.

Extensive research was conducted at the National Archives in College Park, Maryland, the National Cryptologic Museum at Fort Meade and The Women's Army Museum at Fort Lee, VA. The letters written by my mother's commanding officer, Captain Juanita S. Stryker, were found buried in the archives. I reviewed WAC recruiting films and useful military field maps. WWII historians specializing in the Women Army Corps, the Signal Security Agency and the Southwest Pacific Theater, helped me gather invaluable facts and insights.

My research included traveling to specific locations used in the book such as The Commemorative Air Force Museum located on the site of Midland Airfield, Fort Oglethorpe in Georgia and Kellogg, Idaho. I used real names for characters whenever possible including all of Billie Jean's relatives, Nicodemus family members, WACs serving with Billie Jean, crypt-analysts and special services military personal.

The story follows a timeline determined from copies of military orders, dates on letters, genealogical records and chronicled historical accounts. All letters and V-Mails are printed verbatim. Songs and movies were chosen with direct links to the time period. Many of the songs and movie titles I drew from conversations with my parents or from personal memoirs.

I embellished or enhanced verified accounts and family stories in scenes and storylines where I had only a framework in which to draw details. I used my creativity and knowledge of the characters to imagine what might have transpired, creating dialog and expanding scenes to move the story along. I made up names for a few persons known to exist which I could not determine their real names. These individuals were mentioned in stories told to me by my mother, and some were confirmed in letters. There is the occasional fabricated minor character whose existence I felt was necessary for telling an interesting and cohesive story.

Barbara Nicodemus
Knoxville, Tennessee, 2015

About the Author

As a Pediatric Audiologist, Barbara Nicodemus devoted her professional life for over 30 years helping children hear sounds that many take for granted. As a first time author, she is devoted to telling her mother's story, revealing the little known history of the WWII code breaking WACS of the Pacific, a contribution many take for granted.

Barbara moved to Knoxville in 1988 with her husband, Randy Kurth and sons, Forrest and Taylor to take a position in the Audiology Department at the University of Tennessee. She worked in the Early Intervention System and was the consulting audiologist to the TN Department of Health, Newborn Hearing Program before retiring in 2008. Barbara has dedicated herself to empowering others, as a mentor to young professionals and an advisor to parents of special-needs children. She also works with the League of Women Voters to build citizen participation in government. When not traveling with her husband or writing, you might find her behind her loom or kayaking East Tennessee rivers.

Barbara is presently working on her second book, a historical novel set in post war Germany. It will follow the unlikely friendship between an American military family and a German family living in a village outside Munich during the U.S. occupation.

CPSIA information can be obtained at www.ICGtesting.com
Printed in the USA
BVOW08s1937191115

427795BV00004B/92/P